# THE ULTIMATE SOCCER ENCYCLOPEDIA

W9-BYU-745

DAN WOOG

ROXBURY PARK

LOWELL HOUSE JUVENILE

LOS ANGELES

NTC/Contemporary Publishing Group

**Library of Congress Cataloging-in-Publication Data**

Woog, Dan, 1953-
    The ultimate soccer encyclopedia / Dan Woog.
        p.   cm.
    Summary: Brief articles on all aspects of soccer,
including the history of the sport, well known players,
coaches, teams, moves, positions, and techniques.
    ISBN 0-7373-0399-9 (alk. paper)
    1. Soccer—Encyclopedias, Juvenile.
[1. Soccer—Encyclopedias.] I. Title.
    GV943.25 .W66 1999
    796.334'03—dc21

                                                              99-055237

Published by Lowell House
A division of NTC/Contemporary Publishing Group, Inc.
4255 West Touhy Avenue, Lincolnwood (Chicago), Illinois 60712-1975
U.S.A.

Lowell House books can be purchased at special discounts
when ordered in bulk for premiums and special sales.
Contact Department CS at the following address:
NTC/Contemporary Publishing Group
4255 West Touhy Avenue
Lincolnwood, IL 60712-1975
1-800-323-4900

Roxbury Park is a division of
NTC/Contemporary Publishing Group, Inc.

Managing Director and Publisher: Jack Artenstein
Editor in Chief, Roxbury Park Books: Michael Artenstein
Director of Publishing Services: Rena Copperman
Editorial Assistant: Nicole Monastirsky
Interior Designer: Stacie Chaiken
Cover Design: Kristi Mathias
Photos: Allsport

Printed and bound in the United States of America
99  00  01  VP  10  9  8  7  6  5  4  3  2  1

# THE ULTIMATE SOCCER ENCYCLOPEDIA

tion, is the source of frequent soccer injuries.

**AC MILAN:** One of the world's most successful soccer clubs in the late 20th century. Owner Silvio Berlusconi spent freely on international superstars, including Ruud Gullit, Marco Van Basten, Frank Rijkaard, and Franco Baresi.

**ADVANTAGE:** Also called "advantage rule." If, in the referee's judgment, a team that was fouled against is on

**AARONES, ANN KRISTIN:** Offensive star on Norway's 1999 Women's World Cup national team. Scored the only goal (header) in 1995 World Cup semifinal game, which eliminated defending champions U.S. team from tournament.

**ACL:** Anterior cruciate ligament. Helps stabilize the knee but, because soccer demands frequent planting of the foot and changes of direc-

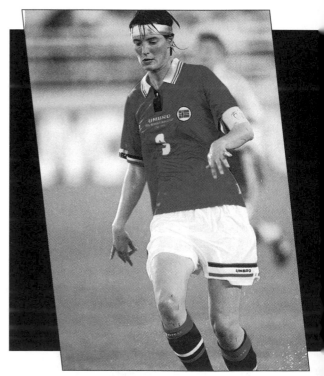

Ann Kristin Aarones

the attack, and would lose an advantage if play were stopped to take a free kick, a referee may allow play to continue.

**AFFILIATION:** Membership by a team or club in a state or national governing body, such as U.S. Soccer. Also, membership by a country in FIFA, the international governing body of soccer.

**FUN SOCCER FACTS**

During an amateur match in Africa in 1998, lightning struck the field of play, killing all 11 players on one team. Ironically, the day before, a "witch doctor" placed a spell on the opposing team.

**AFRICA:** Considered the next major power in world soccer. Teams from Nigeria and Cameroon have performed well at recent World Cups; Nigeria's youth teams are also very strong. South Africa, emerging from a long ban on international competition, should be a force with whom to contend as well. Although no African nation has ever hosted a World Cup, five nations (Nigeria, South Africa, Egypt, Ghana, and Morocco) bid for the 2006 event.

**AFRICAN FOOTBALL CONFEDERATION (CAF):** One of FIFA's six confederations; includes all soccer-playing African nations. Contact information: tel.: 20-2-341-6730; fax: 20-2-342-0114.

**AFRICAN NATIONS' CUP:** National team tournament for African championship; held every two years.

**AGOOS, JEFF:** U.S. national team defender since 1985. Helped lead D.C. United to Major League Soccer titles in 1996 and '97. Four-time All-American at University of Virginia. Current MLS team: D.C. United.

**AJAX:** Pronounced "Eye-ax," this Amsterdam club

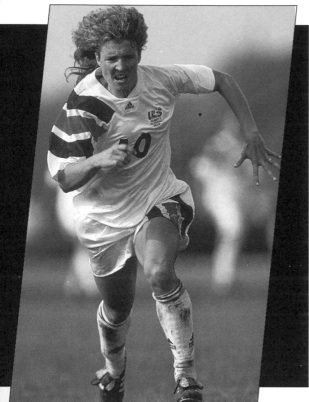

Michelle Akers

the 1980s and '90s, Ajax maintained excellence, despite selling many young stars to Italian clubs.

**AKERS, MICHELLE:** The United States's first female superstar, at both forward and midfield. Tremendous tackling, heading, and passing skills. Scored the first goal ever for the national team (1985); won first Hermann Trophy for women (1988); four-time college All-American (University of Central Florida); produced both American goals in the victorious inaugural Women's World Cup final (1991); earned the first shoe endorsement contract by a female player, and trailed only Mia Hamm in the race to become the leading scorer in soccer history, male or female.

team has won all seven different club championships for which it is eligible. Also (with Juventus) one of only two teams to have won all three European championships. In 1972 they became one of only four teams to sweep the "triple crown" (league, cup, and European championship in one season). In the 1970s, helped popularize "Total Soccer." In

**FOOTNOTE:** Michelle Akers was the first female American player to sign a shoe endorsement contract (1991).

Holds Women's World Cup scoring record with 12 goals. Received Order of Merit, FIFA's highest honor, prior to 1998 World Cup in France; one of only two women to serve on special FIFA commission to help shape future initiatives in soccer. She accomplished all that despite a dozen knee operations and, since 1991, a debilitating bout with Chronic Fatigue Immune Dysfunction Syndrome.

**AKIDE, MERCY:** Nigerian women's national team star; strong offensive threat.

**Bruce Arena**

**A-LEAGUE:** Part of the United Soccer Leagues (USL); the second-highest level of professional soccer in the United States, one step below Major League Soccer.

**ALFONSO:** Spanish national team star; attacking forward. Starred in 1996 European Championships; in 1998 finished second to Ronaldo in Spanish League scoring (25 goals). Full name: Alfonso Perez Muñoz. Current club team: Real Betis (Spain).

**AMERICAN PROFES-SIONAL SOCCER LEAGUE (APSL):** The first professional soccer league in the United States (more accurately, a semiprofessional league). Lasted in various forms from 1921 through 1984.

**AMERICAN YOUTH SOCCER ORGANIZATIONS (AYSO):** Second-largest U.S. youth soccer organization, with more than 560,000 players; also involves 260,000 adults as coaches, referees, and administrators. Founded in 1964; philosophy of "Everyone Plays" mandates everyone play at least half a game, and teams be balanced every year to ensure fair play. Founded 1964; affiliate member of U.S. Soccer Federation. Contact information: 12501 S. Isis Ave., Hawthorne, CA 90250; tel.: 1-800-USA-AYSO; fax: (310) 643-5310; Web site: www.ayso.org.

**ANGLE:** Goalkeeping term. The more a keeper can cut down an angle, by coming off his or her line toward the shooter, the more difficult it is to score.

**ARENA, BRUCE:** Head coach of U.S. men's national team; appointed after disappointing U.S. result at World Cup '98. Selected for his blend of international experience and knowledge of the American system and players, he made an immediate impact. Won five NCAA Division I national championships as head coach at the University of Virginia (1978–95), where he coached numerous national team players and amassed .808 winning percentage; then won first two Major League Soccer titles as head coach of D.C. United. Also won CONCACAF Champions Cup and Interamerican Cup with D.C. United. Previously, coached U.S. Olympic men's team. Played professional soccer (Tacoma Tides, American Soccer League); earned one cap with U.S. national team, as goalkeeper in 2–0 loss to Israel (1973). Also played professional lacrosse (Montreal Quebecois).

**ARGENTINA:** One of the first international soccer powers. Soccer flourished here in the early 1900s, spurred by strong British presence in Buenos Aires. National team formed in 1901; finished second to Uruguay at both the 1928 Olympics and 1930 World Cup. Argentina went into a decline after Italy poached top players for the 1934 World Cup, and did not achieve dominance again until 1978, when it hosted World Cup; won title at home with 3–1 victory over Holland in finals. Argentina won second World Cup in 1986, and was World Cup runner-up in 1990. Argentina handed the United States its first World Cup loss ever, in 1930. Next official meeting came in 1995; the United States won 3–0 in amazing upset, on the way to fourth-place finish at Copa America. In 1999, the United States again won, 1–0, in Washington, D.C.

**ARMAS, CHRIS:** Helped Chicago Fire to MLS championship in first year as franchise; earned call-up to national team.

**Faustino Asprilla**

Kuwait and Saudi Arabia's dominance signaled shift toward Arab states.

**ASIAN FOOTBALL CONFEDERATION (AFC):** One of FIFA's six confederations; includes all Asian soccer-playing nations. Contact information: tel.: 60-3-238-4860; fax: 60-3-238-4862.

**ASPRILLA, FAUSTINO:** Forward; generally considered Colombia's best player. Has had problems with alcohol, unexplained absences, and clashes with coaches. Current club: Palmeiras (Brazil).

**ARSENAL:** A London club that introduced the position of "stopper" to soccer. Nickname ("Gunners") comes from its original base near a South London arsenal.

**ASIAN CUP:** National team tournament; started in 1956, held every four years. Until 1980, dominated by South Korea and Iran. In the 1990s

**ASSISTANT REFEREE:** Also called "linesman." One patrols each side of the field; charged with spotting offside offenses and other infractions the central referee may miss, as well as determining out-of-bounds calls and helping substitutes enter the game.

**ATLANTIC COAST CONFERENCE (ACC):** In men's and women's college soccer, considered for much of the 1990s the premier conference in the country.

**ATLETICO MADRID:** With Real Madrid and Barcelona, part of "Big Three" Spanish clubs.

**AUSTRIA:** Leading soccer power from beginning of 20th century through 1960s, particularly "Wunderteam" of 1931–34.

**AZTECA:** Mexico City stadium; known for intimate seating and intense noise. First stadium to host two World Cup finals (1970, '86). Site of 1968 Olympic final. Capacity: 110,000.

**FUN SOCCER FACTS**

U.S. men's national coach Bruce Arena earned one cap with the U.S. men's national team. He came on the field as a substitute on November 15, 1973, in a 2-1 loss to Israel in Beersheba.

**BADGE:** In the soccer world, badges signify two things: the recipient is certified as either a coach or referee. Badges are awarded by professional organizations, such as FIFA (refereeing), U.S. Soccer and the National Soccer Coaches Association of America, and the English Football Association (coaching).

**BAFANA BAFANA:** Nickname of South African national team.

**BACK DOOR:** The far goal post.

**BACK HEEL:** A pass to a trailing teammate; the ball is kicked backward, using the heel.

**BACK PASS:** Passing the ball to a teammate behind a player, rather than in front or to the side. Because it takes a team farther from the goal they are attacking, a back pass seems counterintuitive. However, the aim is to draw defenders further back to the ball, after which a quick attack forward may be launched.

**BAGGIO, ROBERTO:** Italy's premier player at the 1994 World Cup. During the title game between Italy and Brazil—the first penalty kick shootout ever—blasted Italy's fifth kick over the bar, giving Brazil the world championship. In 1990 Baggio's strike against Czechoslovakia was considered the best goal of the World Cup.

**BAHARMAST, ESSE:** U.S. Soccer director of officials; involved in controversial call at 1998 World Cup when he whistled controversial penalty kick late in Norway's victory over Brazil. Days later, a photograph proved him correct.

**BAHR, WALTER:** Legendary Pennsylvania State University coach; played in historic 1–0 World Cup victory over England, 1950. Elected to U.S. National Soccer Hall of Fame, 1976.

**BALBOA, MARCELO:** In 1995 became the first American to play in 100 international games; currently third on all-time list for most international appearances of any player in the world, and most-capped American ever. A defender, he nonetheless can score; enjoys using the spectacular bicycle kick. Sole two-time winner of U.S. Soccer's Male Athlete of the Year award (1992, '94). Current team: Colorado Rapids.

**BALL:** Basic element of soccer. Can be leather or plastic; stitched (made with a fabric backing) or laminated (glued together). Inner bladder may be made of butyl or latex. Three sizes: 5 (official size for ages 13 and up); 4 (ages 8–12); 3 (under age 8).

**BALL BAG:** Usually mesh; used to carry soccer balls to and from the field.

**BANANA (also called "Banana ball," "banana kick"):** Striking a ball with the outside of the foot, causing it to bend or curve in flight.

**BANKS, GORDON:** English goalkeeper, 1960s and '70s;

Roberto Baggio

helped capture 1966 World Cup title. In the 1970 World Cup match against Brazil, made save on shot by Pele that is considered one of the most amazing in soccer history. Despite losing sight in one eye in a car accident, later starred with Fort Lauderdale Strikers in North American Soccer League.

**BARCELONA:** Spain's top club in the 1990s, with four straight league championships; three achieved in final moments of last day, twice at the expense of archrival Real Madrid. Considered second wealthiest club in world (behind Manchester United). Dutch legend Johan Cruyff played and coached at Barcelona. Home stadium: Nou Camp, one of the most famous in soccer.

Fabien Barthez

**BARTHEZ, FABIEN:** Goalkeeper on France's World Cup–winning team in 1998; won Yashin Prize as best keeper of tournament. Revolutionized position with both flair and fashion sense; feisty, bald, and short-sleeved. Current club team: AS Monaco.

**BATISTUTA, GABRIEL:** Argentine national team star; proven goal scorer. Nicknamed "Bati-goal" for his performance at World Cup '98. Current club team: Fiorentina (Italy).

**David Beckham Lifts
the European Cup**

**BAYERN MUNICH:**
Consistently one of top teams
in German Bundesliga; seemed
set to become first German
team to win European "triple"
in 1999, before conceding two
goals in injury time and losing to Manchester United 2–1
in one of the most remarkable games ever played.

**BEARZOT, ENZO:** Coach of
Italy's 1982 World Cup–
winning team.

**BEAUTIFUL GAME,
THE:** Affectionate
nickname for soccer;
translated from
Brazilian ("O Jogo
Bonito").

**BECKENBAUER,
FRANZ:** Considered
the greatest German
player ever. Called
"The Kaiser" for his
leadership abilities.
At Bayern Munich he
invented the position
of sweeper. Won
World Cup in 1974
with West Germany
as national team cap-
tain, and in 1990 as
coach—the first time anyone
accomplished that feat. Later
became executive vice president of Bayern Munich. Also
gained fame as a teammate
of Pele on the New York
Cosmos. Member of U.S.
National Soccer Hall of Fame.

**BECKHAM, DAVID:** One of
England's top players;
received world attention both
for creative flank midfield
play at Manchester United
(including both corner kick
assists in 1999's storied 2–1

victory over Bayern Munich in European Cup championship), and his marriage to Posh Spice of the Spice Girls. Also known for his temper—red card in 2–2 tie with Argentina in 1998 World Cup is believed by many to have cost England advancement into the next round.

**BELGIUM:** Charter member of FIFA (1904); second-oldest national league (after Britain). However, Belgian soccer did not truly develop until after introduction of full professionalism in 1972.

Dennis Berghamp (Holland) and Roberto Ayala (Argentina) Facing off in the 1998 France World Cup

**BELO HORIZONTE, BRAZIL:** During 1950 World Cup, site of one of the most stunning upsets in soccer history: 1–0 U.S. victory over England. The Americans were a ragtag team; the English were among the best in the world. The goal (header by Joe Gaetjens) was almost a fluke. The Americans lost their next game 5–2 to Chile, and returned home with virtually no publicity.

**BENFICA:** Enormous Lisbon club: 122,000 members, 130,000-seat stadium. Eusebio starred for Benfica in the

1960s. Used only Portuguese players until mid-1970s.

**BERGKAMP, DENNIS:** Explosive striker, all-time leading scorer on Dutch national team. Current club team: Arsenal (England).

**BERLING, CLAY:** Founder of *Soccer America* magazine; elected to U.S. National Hall of Fame, 1995.

**BERNABEU:** Home stadium of Real Madrid; built after Spanish Civil War by former player, coach, and then-president Santiago Bernabeu. Large crowds at Bernabeu enabled Real Madrid to spend lavishly on European stars in the late 1950s and early '60s, and thus dominate European soccer.

**BEST, GEORGE:** Flamboyant English player who led Manchester United to top of European soccer in 1968, 10 years after a plane crash wiped out heart of team. Later played in North American Soccer League.

**BICYCLE KICK:** A spectacular and very difficult shot. With his back to the goal, the shooter leaps up and scissors legs over his head to meet the ball. Called a bicycle kick because it resembles pedaling a bicycle.

**BIERHOFF, OLIVER:** German national team star; potent scorer. Hero of 1996 European Cup championship, with two goals in final match.

Oliver Bierhoff

Current club team: AC Milan (Italy).

**BILARDO, CARLO:** Coach of Argentina's 1986 World Cup–winning team.

**BLADDER:** The inside of a soccer ball. Originally soccer balls were made from the bladder of a cow or sheep. Today bladders are made of rubber or other synthetic materials.

**BLANCHFLOWER, DANNY:** Irish captain in the 1950s and '60s; later, one of the first U.S. soccer broadcasters.

**BLATTER, JOSEPH (SEPP):** President of FIFA, elected to a four-year term prior to the 1998 World Cup in France. A native of Switzerland.

**BOBAN, ZVONIMIR:** Croatian national team star; world-class midfielder, deadly at free kicks. Helped Croatia reach semifinals of their first-ever World Cup (1998). Helped AC Milan to 1994 UEFA Champions' League title, and Serie A championship in 1999. Current club team: AC Milan (Italy).

**BOCA JUNIORS:** One of Buenos Aires's 13 professional clubs, and one of the most famous in the world. Also known for selling Diego Maradona in 1982, after one season, for $5 million to Barcelona. Long dry spell between 1977 and '98, before winning both halves of Argentina's 1998–99 championship.

**BOOTS:** English term for soccer shoes.

**BORGHI, FRANK:** Goalkeeping star of U.S. national team's incredible 1–0 defeat of England in 1950 World Cup. Full-time job: undertaker.

**BOSMAN RULING:** 1995 European Union decision with two major impacts: free agency was granted to players in EU countries at the end of their contracts; and movement of players between EU countries was permitted without restrictions, in accordance with the rights of workers to gain employment in EU nations.

**BRADLEY, BOB:** Assistant coach, U.S. men's national team; also coach of MLS team Chicago Fire. In 1998 led team to MLS Cup title, first time an expansion team in any American sport had won championship its first year. One month later, Fire won U.S. Open Cup. Spent 12 years as Princeton University head coach.

**BRAZIL:** Although soccer was brought to the country at the end of the 19th century by migrant British workers, Brazil soon developed its own distinct style, perhaps the most unique in the world. Teams typically play with flair, flamboyance, and "samba" rhythm; ball control and creativity is unparalleled. Brazil hosted 1950 World Cup; finished runner-up to Uruguay. Won first World Cup in 1958 in Sweden (5–2 over Sweden), as 17-year-old Pele made mark on world. Repeated in 1962 in Chile (3–1 over Czechoslovakia). Became first team ever to win three World Cups, in 1970 in Mexico (4–1 over Italy), with team some consider the best the world has ever seen. Also became first team ever to win four World Cups, in 1994 (on penalty kicks, following 0–0 tie with Italy, in the United States). Runner-up in the 1998 World Cup (3–0 to France). Only country to have played in every World Cup.

Bob Bradley

**BRITISH HOME INTERNATIONAL CHAMPIONSHIP:** Now-dormant tournament among England, Wales, Scotland, and Northern Ireland; the world's first national-team tourney. Discontinued in 1984 because of fan violence.

**BROLIN, TOMAS:** Swedish national team star in 1990s.

**BULGARIA:** Qualified for five of eight World Cups between 1962 and '90, playing 16 matches—and lost all. In post-Communist era, players now in demand in western Europe.

**BUNDESLIGA:** The top division of German soccer.

**BURNS, MIKE:** Sole U.S. player to participate in all four FIFA outdoor world championships (U-17, U-20, Olympics, World Cup); midfielder. Current team: New England Revolution (captain).

**BUSBY, MATT:** Scottish player who took over as coach at Manchester United in 1945, and created legendary teams throughout the '50s. Young "Busby Babes" went twice to European Cup finals before eight were killed in 1958 Munich plane crash. Several surviving "Busby Babes" helped win European Cup in 1968.

## THE WORLD'S GREATEST GAMES
## 1960
**European Cup final: Real Madrid 7, Eintracht Frankfurt 3 (Puskas gets four goals, Di Stefano gets three in front of 135,000 fans)**

Argentina in opening match of 1990 World Cup and reached quarterfinals before bowing in close match to England. Continued strong play at 1994 World Cup. Nickname: "Indomitable Lions."

**CAMPBELL, SOL:** English national team star; defender, dominant in air. Named to 1998 World Cup All-Tournament team. Current club team: Tottenham Hotspur (England).

**CALIGIURI, PAUL:** Scored one of the most important goals ever for U.S. national team: November 19, 1989, in World Cup qualifying match against Trinidad and Tobago. 1–0 win earned the United States the right to play in 1990 tournament, its first World Cup qualification in 40 years. In that '90 World Cup, Caligiuri scored first U.S. World Cup goal since 1950 (versus Czechoslovakia).

**CAMEROON:** Leading African soccer nation; stunned the world by beating reigning champion

**CAMPOS, JORGE:** Flashy goalkeeper; one of first recognizable MLS stars. Left Chicago Fire after losing starting position to Zach Thornton; returned to play in native Mexico.

**CANADA:** Weak soccer nation. Problems include weather; its enormous size; and popularity of hockey, baseball, basketball, and football.

**CANADIAN SOCCER ASSO-CIATION:** Governing body responsible for all soccer in

Canada. Contact information: tel.: 613-237-7678; fax: 613-237-1516.

**CANTONA, ERIC:** A Frenchman who at Manchester United was considered one of the best players in English soccer since Sir Stanley Matthews and Gordon Banks 30 years earlier. In 1994 he became the first foreigner ever named England's Football Player of the Year.
Career was marred by several in-stances of poor sportsmanship, including assault of a fan.

**CANTOR, ANDRES:** Most famous soccer announcer in American history. World Cup viewers forsake English-language stations for Cantor's Spanish-language broadcasts, especially his exciting, elongated "Goooooooolllllllllll!!!!!!!" call.

**CAP:** Name for each appearance a player makes with his full national team, in interna-

Song, playing for Cameroon 1998 Coupe du Monde

tional competition. Originally, players were awarded for appearances with actual "caps"; today the word is a mere formality.

**CAPTAIN:** The on-field leader of a team. In youth soccer, teams can have more than one captain on the field; in international soccer, only one captain is allowed. The captain handles most communication between the referee and other players.

**CAPTAIN'S BAND:** Armband worn by the captain, to indicate his or her status to the referee.

**CARBAJAL, ANTONIO:** Mexican goalkeeper; first player to play in five consecutive World Cups (1950–66).

**CARLOS ALBERTO:** Brazilian sweeper; in 1970s one of the best defenders in the world. Played on glamorous Cosmos teams in the late '70s.

**CATENACCIO:** Italian style of defense, most popular in the 1970s; critics termed it "sterile," reflecting philosophy that not losing is more important than winning.

**CAUTION:** A referee may "caution" a player verbally, or by issuing a yellow card. It is expected that a caution will cause a cessation of a particular offense; otherwise, a more serious penalty may result.

**CELTIC:** Glasgow club; with Rangers, half of one of soccer's greatest rivalries. One of only four clubs to have swept "triple crown" (league, cup, and European championship) in one season (1967). Founded in 1888; long known as Glasgow's Catholic team.

**CENTER:** A player who plays in the middle of his area (center forward, center midfielder, center fullback). The more modern term is "central."

**CENTER CIRCLE:** The center circle, with a 10-yard radius, designates the area from which a team kicks off.

Eric Cantona

All opponents must stand outside the circle.

**CENTRAL:** A player who plays in the middle of his area (central midfielder, central defender).

**CHAMPIONS LEAGUE:** Annual European tournament involving 32 club teams (league champions and, in top soccer countries, up to three other runner-up teams).

**CHARGING:** Illegally running at an opponent, without attempting to win the ball. Charging foul results in a direct kick for the other team.

**CHARLES, CLIVE:** Head coach, U.S. men's U-23 national team; also head coach, men's and women's teams, University of Portland.

**CHARLTON, BOBBY:** English star of the 1950s and '60s; survivor of 1958 Munich air crash who helped lead England to 1966 World Cup victory, and Manchester United to 1968 European Cup title. Known for high standards of sportsmanship. Brother of Jack.

**CHARLTON, JACK:** English star of the 1950s and '60s; helped lead England to 1966 World Cup victory. Brother of Bobby.

**CHASTAIN, BRANDI:** U.S. women's national team star who played in 1991 and '99 Women's World Cups; scored final penalty kick to give her

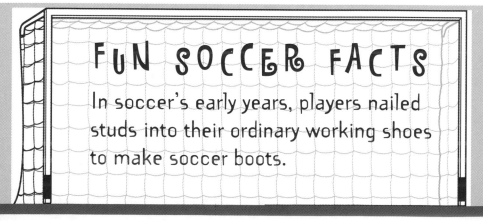

**FUN SOCCER FACTS**

In soccer's early years, players nailed studs into their ordinary working shoes to make soccer boots.

team the '99 title. Excellent as attacker and defender; now primarily plays midfield. Husband, Jerry Smith, coaches women's team (and was her coach) at Santa Clara University.

**CHEST TRAP:** Controlling the ball by arching back and letting it bounce from the chest to ground (or foot).

**CHICAGO FIRE:** Expansion team (1998) in Major League Soccer (MLS). Made American sports history by winning MLS Cup league championship in first year of existence; amazingly, accomplished feat by beating two-time champion D.C. United. Fire then won "double" by beating Columbus Crew 2–1 in U.S. Open Cup final.

**CHILAVERT, JOSÉ LUIS:** Paraguayan national team goalkeeper; largely responsible for team reaching second round in 1998 World Cup, giving up only two goals in four games. Named to All-Tourna-

**Brandi Chastain**

ment team. Known for booming kicks and loud mouth. Recently banned from club soccer in Argentina for assaulting a stadium official. Current club team: Velez Sarsfield (Argentina).

**CHILE:** Hosted 1962 World Cup (won by Brazil).

**CHINA:** Site of inaugural Women's World Cup in 1991; 60,000 fans watched finals. China fields one of the top women's soccer teams in the

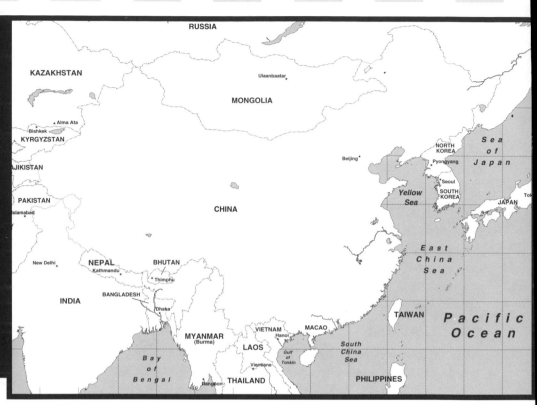

## China

world; finished second to the United States in 1999 Women's World Cup, falling 5–4 in penalty kicks after 120 minutes of scoreless play.

**CHINAGLIA, GIORGIO:** So-so Italian player with Lazio; made name with North American Soccer League Cosmos as vaunted goal scorer.

**CHIP:** A pass of medium length, in the air.

**CHONDROMALACIA:** Growth disease (softening of cartilage around knee) that can affect teenage soccer players.

**CHUNG, MARK:** All-time MLS leader in games played. Current MLS team: New York/New Jersey MetroStars.

**CHYZOWYCH, WALTER:** Legendary coach at all levels in the United States; national team coach, 1976–80. Elected to U.S. National Hall of Fame, 1997.

**CLASSIC SOCCER:** In youth soccer, a competitive team or league—but usually not the highest level.

**"CLEAR IT!":** Call by goal-keeper or defender, instructing a player to knock the ball as far away as possible.

**CLEATS:** Though sometimes used to refer to soccer shoes, "cleats" are actually the studs on the bottom of shoes that give players traction on grass.

**"CLOCKWORK ORANGE":** Nickname of great Dutch teams of the 1970s (see "Holland").

**CLUBS:** The foundation of soccer throughout the world. Clubs sponsor teams at various age groups, from professional to youth; overseas, all teams in a club usually share playing philosophy, facilities, and team colors. In the United States, soccer clubs are less developed; many youth teams may play under a club banner, but share little else—not even common playing fields. It is extremely rare for U.S. youth clubs to be affiliated with professional teams.

**COACH:** Leader of a soccer team;

Mark Chung

the English word for coach is "manager." Unlike many sports, a soccer coach has little impact on a team once a match begins; there are too few substitutions, and no time-outs. A coach's main influence comes during training sessions.

**COERVER COACHING METHOD:** Popular method of youth soccer instruction that emphasizes individual ball skills and moves.

**COLLEGE CUP:** As of 1999 new name for men's and women's NCAA Division I college championships.

**COLO COLO:** Chilean club; traditionally one of the best in South America.

**COLOMBIA:** In the 1990s, emerged as challenger to Argentina and Brazil in South America, but never reached its potential.

**COLORADO RAPIDS:** Denver-based team; charter member of Major League Soccer (MLS).

**COLUMBUS CREW:** Charter member of Major League Soccer (MLS). Smallest market in league, but received national attention in 1999 when team opened Columbus Crew Stadium, the first soccer-specific major facility in the United States. Seats 22,500; built in nine months at a cost of $28.5 million.

# THE WORLD'S GREATEST GAMES
## 1970

**World Cup semifinal: Italy 4, West Germany 3**
**(West Germans equalize 1–1 late in game; then a**
**scoring rampage in overtime, until Rivera clinches match)**

**CONCACAF (Confederation of North and Central American and Caribbean Football):** One of FIFA's six confederations; founded in 1961, includes all 38 soccer-playing nations in North and Central America and the Caribbean, including the United States. CONCACAF organizes international competitions that include Champions' Cup (won in 1998 by D.C. United); women's, veterans, and youth championships; qualifying tournaments for all FIFA competitions (including World Cup); and biannual Gold Cup, CONCACAF's showcase event that determines confederation champion. Headquarters: New York City. Current president: Jack Warner of Trinidad and Tobago. Contact information: tel.: 212-308-0044; fax: 212-308-1851.

**CONES:** Rubber devices used as a fundamental training device. Cones can be set up to designate boundaries and serve as goals, even as obstacle courses to develop dribbling skills. When a team wins an easy game against a weak opponent that moves poorly, losing players are said to have "played like cones."

**CONDITIONING:** Cardio-vascular fitness training.

**CONFEDERATION:** Six divisions into which FIFA divides the world, for administrative purposes: CONCACAF (North and Central America and the Caribbean); UEFA (Europe); CAF (Africa); AFC (Asia); CONMEBOL (South America); and Oceania.

**CONFEDERATIONS CUP:** Tournament pitting champions of each FIFA confederation against each other.

**"CONTAIN!":** Call made to fellow defender to slow down an opposing attacker, giving the rest of the defenders time to run back and get in position.

**CONTIGUGLIA, DR. S. ROBERT:** President of U.S. Soccer; elected August 22, 1998. Previously chairman of U.S. Youth Soccer (1990–96); also an All-Ivy League player

(Columbia University) and U.S. Soccer A-licensed coach. President of Colorado Kidney Associates in Denver.

**CONTINENTAL INDOOR SOCCER LEAGUE:** Minor league. Began play 1993 with seven teams; folded in 1997.

**CONTROL:** Formerly called "trap"; refers to the ability of soccer players to handle a ball with any part of the body, including head, chest, thigh, and foot. "Control" is favored over "trap" because latter term seems too stagnant for a fluid game.

**COOL DOWN:** Jogging and stretching after a match or training.

**COPA AMERICA:** Tournament for national teams in CONMEBOL (South American) confederation of FIFA; non–South American teams occasionally invited. Oldest of all national-team tournaments; began 1916, predating European championship by 50 years. After irregular scheduling, now held every two years.

**COPA LIBERTADORES:** South America's premier club competition, involving champions of various countries; started in 1960. Format, including final, is home-and-home series.

**CORNER ARC (also called "Corner circle"):** Quarter-circle one yard in diameter on each corner of the field, designating spot from which a corner kick may be taken.

**CORNER FLAG:** Five-foot-high flag designating each corner of the field. Flags bend when struck; for purposes of play, considered part of the field.

**CORNER KICK:** When a defensive team kicks the ball over its own end line, opponents receive a corner kick, taken from corner arc on the side of the field where the ball went out. A corner kick is direct; a goal may be scored directly, without any other player touching the ball.

**COSMOS:** In the 1970s one of the most famous clubs in the world. The Cosmos leapt from obscurity of North American Soccer League to international fame in 1975, when the team coaxed Pele out of a three-year retirement. The move gave the league instant credibility. The Cosmos, who moved to New Jersey's Giants Stadium in 1977, also signed international superstars (Franz Beckenbauer, Giorgio Chinaglia, Carlos Alberto, and Johan Neeskens), and toured the world. However, glamorous lineup and high salaries opened up the gulf between the Cosmos and the rest of the league, which hastened its demise in 1985.

**COUNTERATTACK (also called a "Counter"):** Quick attack upfield by a team that moments before had been on defense. Good counterattacks occur when one team steals the ball from the other, catching all opponents moving forward, unmindful of playing defense.

**CRAMER, DETTMAR:** German coach; former U.S. national team coach, founded U.S. Soccer's Coaching Department (license program) in the early 1970s.

**CROSS:** Long pass in the air from one side of the field to middle, usually used to set up shot on goal.

**CROSSBAR:** Horizontal, eight-yard-long bar that connects two goal posts at top. Crossbars were originally made of wood; now, most are aluminum.

**CRUYFF, JOHAN:** Centerpiece of great Dutch teams of the

Johan Cruyff

1970s; epitomized "Total Soccer." Started at center forward, but could also be found in midfield and on flanks. Named European Football Player of the Year three times. Although most closely associated with Ajax and Barcelona, as both player and coach, also played with Los Angeles Aztecs and Washington Diplomats of the North American Soccer League.

**CUBILLAS, TEOFILO:** Peruvian national team star; scored 10 goals in 1970 and '78 World Cups. Also starred for Fort Lauderdale Strikers of the North American Soccer League.

**CUP:** Trophy or tournament.

**CUP WINNERS' CUP:** Competition in which the winner of a country's domestic cup competition faces counterparts from neighboring countries. In Europe, suspended in 2000 due to growth of other competitions.

**CZECHOSLOVAKIA:** Two-time World Cup runner-up (1934, 2–1 in overtime to Italy; 1962, 3–1 to Brazil). Breakup of country after Communist era hurt national team's prospects.

# THE WORLD'S GREATEST GAMES
## 1930
### World Cup final: Uruguay 4, Argentina 2
### (First World Cup final sets high standard for excitement)

judgment, endangers safety of any player—including the one committing the infraction (in other words, a player attempting to head a low ball may be called for dangerous play for putting himself in danger, just as one who attempts a dangerous kick with others nearby may be called for the infraction). When dangerous play is called, the other team receives an indirect kick.

**DALGLISH, KENNY:** Scottish star; won 25 major trophies as player and coach (Celtic and Liverpool).

**DALLAS BURN:** Charter member of Major League Soccer (MLS).

**DALLAS CUP:** Youth tournament held each Easter in Texas; top international club teams participate. Considered to be the most prestigious youth tournament in the United States.

**DANGEROUS PLAY:** Any action that, in the referee's

**DASHER BOARDS:** Side boards in indoor soccer. As in ice hockey, players may use the boards for "wall passes"; unlike hockey, however, players may not be checked into dasher boards.

**DAVIDS, EDGAR:** Dutch national team star at 1998 World Cup; named to All-Tournament team. Defensive midfielder; nicknamed "Pit Bull" for hard tackles and aggressive play. Current club team: Juventus (Italy).

**DAVIS, RICKY:** With Kyle Rote Jr., first American-born soccer star. In the 1970s and early '80s, played on U.S. national team and with Cosmos.

**D.C. UNITED:** Based in Washington, D.C. Champions first two years of Major League Soccer (MLS), 1996–97; reached MLS Cup final in '98, but lost to Chicago Fire.

**DEAD BALL:** A ball not in play because it is out of bounds or on the ground, awaiting a restart.

**DE BOER, FRANK:** Captain of Dutch national team; made 1998 World Cup All-Tournament team. In 1996 helped lead Ajax to UEFA Champions' League title. Central defender. Twin brother, Ronald, also national team star. Current club team: Barcelona (Spain).

**DE BOER, RONALD:** Dutch national team star; with twin brother, Frank, helped Ajax win UEFA

Champions' League title. Versatile attacking midfielder. Current club team: Barcelona (Spain).

**DECOY:** A teammate who appears ready to receive a pass, but does not. By attracting defenders, a decoy opens up space on the field for teammates to run into.

**DEFENDER:** Player whose primary job is to prevent offensive penetration, win the ball, and initiate attack.

Ronald De Boer

Defenders are also called "fullbacks." Position includes outside (flank) defender, central defender, sweeper, and stopper. Most modern teams play with three or four defenders.

**DEFENSE:** Any time a team loses the ball, they are on the defense. In soccer, all players on the team without the ball are said to be playing defense, even if their position is striker.

**DEFENSIVE WALL:** See "wall."

**DELAY OF GAME:** Soccer players are expected to keep play moving. Goalkeepers may be called for delay of game for failing to put ball into play in a timely manner (usually 5–6 seconds) after a save. Field players may be called for delay of game for stalling tactics (taking too much time to set up a free kick, failing to move back while setting up defensive wall, constantly changing players before taking throw-in, etc.). When a player is called for delay of game, opposition is awarded an indirect kick.

**DEL PIERO, ALESSANDRO:** Italian national team star; powerful forward with dangerous free kick. Scored important goals at World Cup '98, Euro '96, and in Champions League play. Current club team: Juventus (Italy).

**DENILSON:** Brazilian national team star; one of the most creative, undefendable players in the world. Became world's most expensive player when sold from Sao Paulo to current club team, Spain's Real Betis, for transfer fee of £46 million. Full name: Denilson de Oliveira.

**DENMARK:** Charter member of FIFA (1904); however, adherence to amateurism has held back soccer growth. In 1992 stunned the world by winning European Championship—especially remarkable because team was a late replacement after Yugoslavia

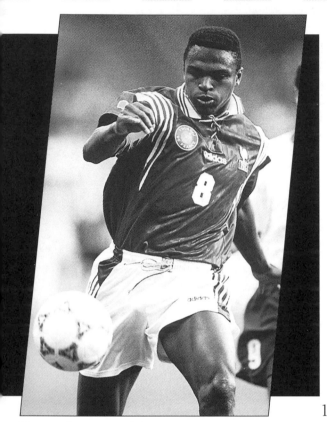

Marcel Desailly

World Cup–winning team; helped Juventus win '96 European Cup. Current club team: Chelsea (England).

**DIAZ ARCE, RAUL:** MLS star. After three years, led league in both points and goals. Current MLS team: Tampa Bay Mutiny.

**DI CICCO, TONY:** Since 1994 head coach of U.S. women's national team; winningest women's coach in U.S. national team history. In 1999, led the United States to Women's World Cup championship; in '96 coached the United States to gold medal in first-ever Olympic women's soccer. Former assistant national team coach to Anson Dorrance; has also served as goalkeeper coach for U-20 men's national team. Brief stint with U.S. national team (1973).

was expelled, and competed with minimal training.

**DESAILLY, MARCEL:** Fearsome defender on France's 1998 World Cup–winning team. Won two UEFA Champions' League titles (OM Marseille, AC Milan). Current club team: Chelsea (England).

**DESCHAMPS, DIDIER:** Captain of France's 1998

**DIDI:** Midfield general on great Brazilian national teams of the 1950s and early '60s.

Known for amazingly accurate free kicks.

**DI MATTEO, ROBERTO:**
Italian national team star; midfielder with great passing skills. Current club team: Chelsea (England).

**DIRECT KICK:** A free kick awarded after a foul involving physical contact or a hand ball. Examples of direct kick fouls: kicking, tripping, jumping at, charging, spitting at, striking, holding or pushing an opponent, or committing a violent tackle. A direct kick may be scored "directly" from the kick; no other player needs to touch the ball. All defenders must stand at least 10 yards from the ball. Direct kick foul committed by defensive team within penalty area results in a penalty kick (see "penalty kick").

**DISSENT:** Disagreement with a referee's decision; may be expressed verbally or physically. Punishment for dissent includes yellow or red card.

**DI STEFANO, ALFREDO:**
Spanish star of the 1950s and early '60s. Dominated European soccer; considered by many to be the best player of all time, Pele notwithstanding. Led Real Madrid to victory in first five European Cup finals; later coached in Argentina and Spain.

**DISTRIBUTION:** Getting rid of ball to a teammate; usually refers to goalkeeper's kick or throw.

**DIVE:** Falling intentionally, usually in the penalty box, following a slight nudge, in hopes of convincing referee that a foul occurred. At the

FUN SOCCER FACTS

Although American television ignored it, soccer was the most popular sport at the 1996 Olympics in Atlanta.

end of the 1990s, FIFA instructed officials to take stern action against diving.

**DIVING HEADER:** A dramatic shot or defensive clearance, in which the player heading the ball extends parallel to the ground, and strongly drives the ball forward.

**DJORKAEFF, YOURI:** Member of France's 1998 World Cup–winning team.

**DODD, MARK:** One of the first MLS goalkeeping stars. After three years with Dallas Burn, led league in wins; was second in shutouts.

**DONNELLY CUP:** Annual national championship for amateur state select teams; named for George F. Donnelly.

**DONOVAN, LANDON:** Highly touted U.S. national youth team star; considered best American youth prospect. Current club team: Bayer Leverkusen (Germany).

**DOOLEY, THOMAS:** Son of U.S. Army veteran who married a German woman, he was raised in Germany, and played professional soccer there. In 1992 learned he was eligible to play for U.S. national team, and became an American citizen. Quickly became a fixture on the U.S. squad, and in 1993 was named U.S. Soccer Male Athlete of the Year. Cap-

Youri Djorkaeff

Thomas Dooley

women) from UNC. National team record: 65–22–5.

**DOUBLE:** Winning two major championships in one year (for example, English Football League and F.A. Cup).

**"DOWN LINE!":** Command to a teammate to pass the ball upfield, as close to sideline as possible.

tained U.S. World Cup team in 1998. Current MLS team: Colum-bus Crew.

**DORRANCE, ANSON:** Legendary women's coach at University of North Carolina; former coach of U.S. national team (1986–94). Also coached University of North Carolina men's team, and received law degree (while simultaneously coaching both the men and

**DRIBBLING:** Controlling the ball with the feet, while running.

**"DRIVE IT!":** Command used to indicate teammate should hit a ball hard and low.

**DROP BALL:** Method of restarting play, if the referee cannot tell which team kicked it out of bounds, or after simultaneous fouls by both teams. Referee drops ball between two opponents; as soon as it hits the ground, it is in play.

**DROP KICK:** Punt in which a keeper drops the ball directly on the foot, then bangs it upfield.

**D3 PRO LEAGUE:** Division III professional league in the United States; part of the United Soccer Leagues (USL). One step below the A-League.

**DUCAR, TRACY:** U.S. women's national team goalkeeper; led University of North Carolina to NCAA championship in 1994, and Raleigh Wings to 1998 W-League title.

**"DUMMY RUN":** A Dummy run occurs when a player receiving a pass lets the ball run between his legs, so it reaches another teammate. Defenders assume first player will pick it up; when he does not, but the second player does, defenders may be caught off guard.

**DUNGA:** Longtime Brazilian star defender; captain of 1994 World Cup championship team.

**DYNAMO KIEV:** First Soviet team to win a European championship (1975); now the pride of the Ukraine.

**Dunga with Team and Trophy, 7/17/94**

entirely over end line to count as a goal. Goal line must be no shorter than 50 yards wide, and no longer than 100 yards wide.

**ENGLAND:** Country that founded soccer; game developed on school fields in the mid-19th century, was then codified and organized during 1860s. England participated in first international match, against Scotland in Glasgow (1872). Professional league organized in 1888. Country became more isolated after World War I; withdrew from FIFA in 1920 in order not to play against wartime foes. England was humbled by 1–0 World Cup loss to the United States in 1950, and 6–3 defeat at Wembley to Hungary in 1953 (first-ever defeat to non-British team at home). England hosted 1966 World Cup, and won it with storybook 4–2 overtime win over West Germany at Wembley; team was dubbed the "wingless wonders," for straightforward style of play. England's club teams went on to great European success through the mid-'80s, but the national

**EJECTION:** See "Red Card."

**ELEVEN:** Number of players on the field in a regulation soccer game; number may be lower due to injuries or ejections. Seven players must be on field for match to begin.

**ELLINGER, JOHN:** Head coach, U.S. men's U-17 national team.

**END LINE:** The boundary line extending from one side of field to the other; also called "goal line." Ball must be entirely over end line to be out of bounds; if shot between goal posts, must go team never again achieved great heights. Failure to qualify for 1994 World Cup seen as tremendous blow to national pride, as was hooliganism that led to stadium tragedies in 1985 and '89.

**ENGLISH LEAGUE:** The biggest professional league in the world (92 teams in four divisions). Top division is Premier; then comes First, Second, and Third Divisions.

**ENRIQUE, LUIS:** Spanish national team star; helped win gold medal at 1992 Olympics in Barcelona. Versatile play maker. Current club team: Barcelona (Spain).

**ESCOBAR, ANDRES:** Colombian defender who scored own goal in 2–1 loss to United States at 1994 World Cup; gunned down by unknown assailants a few days after returning home to Medellin.

**ETCHEVERRY, MARCO:** One of the first MLS stars, with D.C. United; after three years, led league in assists.

**EUROPE:** With South America, one of the world's two leading soccer continents. Professional soccer began in the 1920s; importation of foreign stars started in the '30s. Growth exploded after World War I, and has continued unabated since.

**EUROPEAN CHAMPIONSHIP:** Most prestigious championship in Europe; held every four years; surprisingly, last of European championships to get established (1960). After qualifying rounds, includes top 16 European national teams. "Euro 2000" held in Belgium and the Netherlands.

**EUROPEAN CUP:** Annual tournament held to determine the champion of all of Europe's national champions; considered the continent's premier club event. Begun in 1956. Format is home-and-home on a knockout basis—except the final (single match at a neutral site).

**EUROPEAN CUP–WINNERS' CUP:** Annual

competition for winners of national knockout competitions; begun in 1963. Home-and-away matches played until finals, which is now a single match. Considered least important of Europe's three major competitions, but

allows some of Europe's smaller clubs a chance at glory.

**EUSEBIO:** The "Black Pearl"; quick, strong player who grew up in Mozambique and became first African superstar. Spent 13 seasons with Benfica; won seven Portuguese championships. Was named European Football Player of the Year in 1965; arguably best player at 1966 World Cup. Eusebio ended his career in the North American Soccer League.

1966 World Cup Semi Finals Eusebio in Tears England v. Portugal

**F.A.:** Football Association; the ruling body of English soccer.

**F.A. CUP:** The premier knockout competition in England; introduced in 1871, is both the first and oldest surviving tournament in the soccer world.

**FAIR PLAY:** Slogan popularized by FIFA to draw attention to the importance of sportsmanship in soccer. "Fair Play Award" is given in major tournaments; at 1998 World Cup, shared by France and England.

**FAKE:** Move used to trick an opponent; also called a "feint."

**FAROE ISLANDS:** Tiny European nation stunned world at 1992 European Championship with 1–0 win over Austria, in its first competitive match ever.

**FAR POST:** The goalpost farthest away from the shooter or defender.

**FAWCETT, JOY:** U.S. women's national team star who played in 1991, '95, and '99 Women's World Cups; scored penalty kick to help team win '99 title. Backfield stalwart, unafraid to go forward; considered by some to be the world's best defender. Named UCLA's first women's soccer coach in 1993. Took time off from soccer to have two daughters, but her endurance never suffered.

**FERGUSON, ALEX:** Manchester United coach; like fellow Scotsman Sir Matt Busby, won European Cup championship (1999) in 13th year with club, and was subsequently knighted by queen.

**FIELD:** A soccer field is rectangular (cannot be square); must be between 100 and 130 yards long, and 50 and 100 yards wide. Center of field has a midline stripe; circle with 10-yard radius marks where the players are positioned during kickoffs. At each end is a goal (8 yards high, 8 yards wide); in front of each goal is a penalty area, extending 18 yards from end line and measuring 44 yards across; goalkeeper can handle ball inside this area. Inside penalty area is a smaller (6 yards long, 10 yards wide) goal area, from which goal kicks are taken. Penalty spot, 10 yards from goal, marks area from which penalty kicks are taken. Small penalty arc keeps players 10 yards from penalty spot. At each corner is a small quarter-circle with 1-yard radius, for corner kicks. There are goals at each end, flags at least five feet high at each corner, and sometimes flags at midfield. Note: The English call a soccer field a "pitch."

**FIELD PLAYER:** Any player other than the goalkeeper.

**FIFA:** Acronym for Fédération Internationale de Football Association; the international governing body of soccer. All countries wishing to compete for World Cup must belong to FIFA, and abide by its laws (at the turn of the millennium, that num-

## THE WORLD'S GREATEST GAMES
## 1953

Friendly: Hungary 6, England 3: First time England lost at home to non–British team; set scene for shift of soccer power from England to continental Europe

# FUN SOCCER FACTS

Goalkeepers did not have to wear distinctive colors until 1913. Prior to that, they were distinguished from their teammates only by a cap. It was not until the 1980s that keepers were allowed to wear a color other than green, yellow, or white.

ber was 203). As soccer's ultimate administrative authority, FIFA governs all facets of play, including rules, transfers, international competitions, referee standards, sports medicine, and development. FIFA sponsors quadrennial World Cup championships for men and women, as well as World Championships for male and female youth teams; biannual FIFA Confederations Cup between each of its six confederations' (UEFA, Oceania, CONMEBOL, CONCACAF, CAF, and AFC) champions; and, beginning in 2000, World Club Championship. FIFA was founded in 1904, with charter members France, Belgium, Denmark, Netherlands, Spain, Sweden, and Switzerland; is now headquartered in Geneva, Switzerland. Contact information: P.O. Box 85, 8030 Zurich, Switzerland, tel.: 41-1-384-9595; fax: 41-1-384-9696; Web site: www.fifa.com.

**FIGO, LUIS:** Portuguese national team star; flashy dribbler, strong midfielder. Captain of Barcelona. Nickname: "Captain Catalan."

**FINISH:** To score a goal. An adept goal scorer is a "finisher"; scoring is called "finishing." A particularly fine goal is greeted with "great finish!"; a spectacular one with "brilliant finish!"

**FLAMENGO:** With Fluminense, half of an excellent Rio de Janeiro rivalry.

**FLANK:** Outside of the field; also called "wing."

**"FLATS":** Nickname given to soccer shoes used for indoor training.

**FLICK HEADER:** A pass in which a player quickly "flicks" ball with his head to nearby teammate.

**FLICK PASS:** A pass using outside of the foot; the ball is usually flicked past opponent.

**FLUMINENSE:** A Rio de Janeiro, Brazil, team; their stadium, Maracana, is among the most famous in the world. Crosstown rival: Flamengo.

**FONTAINE, JUST:** French star of the 1950s; scored 13 goals at 1958 World Cup. Retired prematurely in 1961 after two double leg fractures. Briefly served as national team coach.

**FOOTBALL:** What soccer is called in many parts of

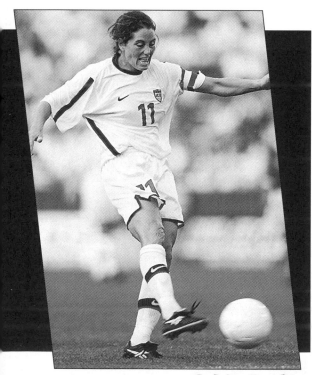

Julie Foudy

the world. (Makes sense, because game is played primarily with feet.)

**FORWARD:** Position on offensive line. Primary job is to score, and assist on goals; however, most forwards are also expected to win balls from defenders in offensive third of the field. Position is also called "striker."

**FOTOPOULOS, DANIELLE:** U.S. national team player; fast attacker. Scored winning goal in 1998 NCAA final for University of Florida against North Carolina; set all-time NCAA scoring record, male or female (118 goals).

**FOUDY, JULIE:** U.S. women's national team star who played in 1991, '95, and '99 Women's World Cups; cocaptain in '99. Joined national team at age 17. A vocal leader who became greater offensive threat toward end of '90s as attacking midfielder. Served as ESPN television announcer during men's 1998 World

**FUN SOCCER FACTS**

The United States and Iran were both honored with the 1998 FIFA Fair Play Award for their display of sportsmanship during their World Cup encounter on FIFA Fair Play Day.

Cup. First woman and first American to receive FIFA Fair Play Award (1997, for work against child labor in soccer manufacturing). Accepted into Stanford University Medical School, but decided not to pursue medicine.

**FOUL:** Infraction committed against opponent. There are two types of fouls (see "direct kick" and "indirect kick").

**FOULDS, SAM:** Longtime U.S. soccer historian; elected to U.S. National Soccer Hall of Fame, 1969.

**FRANCE:** Long considered a second-tier soccer nation (at least by European standards), France hosted the 1998 World Cup—then stunned globe by winning entire tournament. Final match was decisive 3–0 victory over Brazil. Also hosted 1938 World Cup (winner: Italy). Charter member of FIFA (1904); prime movers behind creation of FIFA, UEFA, World Cup, and European Championship.

**FRANCE FOOTBALL:** French soccer magazine; one of the leading soccer publications in the world.

**FREE KICK:** Kick awarded to opposite team after a foul. Free kicks may be either direct or indirect (see "direct kick" and "indirect kick").

**FRICKER, WERNER:** Longtime U.S. soccer administrator; elected to U.S. National Soccer Hall of Fame, 1992.

**FRIEDEL, BRAD:** 6′4″ goalkeeper for U.S. national team; three greatest appearances have come against archrival Mexico. One of top goalkeepers in European soccer, with English club Liverpool. In 1993 as a junior at UCLA, won Hermann Trophy, given to top college soccer player in country. Current club team: Liverpool (England).

**FRIENDLY:** An exhibition game, in which result does not count for anything.

**FUTBOL:** Spanish word for "football" (see "football").

**FUTSAL:** Five-a-side version of indoor soccer, played on basketball-style court but without walls; free substitution. U.S. men have experienced more success in futsal than any outdoor FIFA competition (two Top 3 finishes in world championships). U.S. governing body (U.S. Futsal Federation) contact information: tel.: 1-800-5-FUTSAL; fax: (510) 527-8110.

**GANSLER, BOB:** Coach of the U.S. national team in 1982 and 1989–91; in 1990 took the United States to first World Cup in 40 years. Hungarian born, but a longtime Milwaukee resident with knowledge of American soccer. In 1999, named coach of MLS team Kansas City Wizards.

**GAO HONG:** Goalkeeping star on China's 1999 women's national team.

**GABARRA, CARIN JEN-NINGS:** Star of U.S. national women's team, 1987–96; 52 goals in 117 games. Selected as Golden Ball (Most Valuable Player) winner of 1991 Women's World Cup.

**GAETJENS, JOE:** In 1950 he scored the most famous goal in American soccer history: a header in the United States 1–0 World Cup victory over England in Belo Horizonte, Brazil. A postal worker, he later returned to his native Haiti and was believed murdered by a political group. Elected to U.S. National Soccer Hall of Fame, 1976.

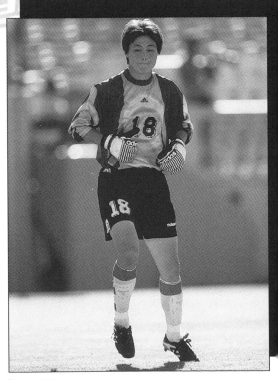

Gao Hong

**GARBER, DON:** Second commissioner of Major League Soccer (appointed August 1999). Background: NFL Europe.

**GARDNER, PAUL:** Long-time columnist for *Soccer America* magazine, book author, and television commentator; considered one of the keenest observers of the world soccer scene. Although English, is strong advocate of South American soccer and, in the United States, greater participation by Latinos and inner-city youths.

**GARRINCHA:** Star of the 1950s who, before Pele, was considered the greatest Brazilian soccer player ever. Legs badly twisted because of childhood illness; doctors thought he might never walk, but became one of the quickest and most dangerous right wings of all time. Died prematurely of alcoholism.

**GASCOIGNE, PAUL:** Mercurial English star of the 1990s; as famous for bursting into tears during a World Cup match as for exceptional, if seldom-realized, talent.

**GEBAUER, WENDY:** Former U.S. women's national team member; first female to play in a U.S. men's Division II professional game (1999, for A-League Raleigh Capital Express in 3–0 loss to Boston Bulldogs). Current W-League team: Raleigh Wings.

**GERMANY:** Since the end of World War II, West German (now German) teams have enjoyed tremendous success; characterized by discipline, physical strength, and great determination. World Cup semifinalists (1958), quarterfinalists ('62), runners-up ('66); won World Cup '74. Also fields strong women's national team (1995 Women's World Cup runners-up).

**"GET STUCK IN!":** Popular request of coaches and fans. Meaning: "Go in hard! Tackle aggressively! Don't be afraid of the ball or opponent!"

**GIGGS, RYAN:** Flank midfielder, speedy down wing

and extremely dangerous one-on-one. Passed up opportunity to play for England, instead choosing homeland of Wales. Current club team: Manchester United (England).

**GIVE-AND-GO:** Pass in which one player acts as a "wall"; after receiving ball, he immediately one-touches it to player who gave it to him. Also called "wall pass" or "one-two."

**GLOVES:** Used by goalkeepers; today's gloves have large, adhesive surface areas to enhance saving ability.

**GOAL:** Object of soccer is to score a goal. Seems straightforward—putting the ball into the net—but besides presence of defenders and goalkeepers, there is one other difficulty: the whole ball must cross the entire line in order for a goal to count. The goal itself measures 8 feet high by 8 yards wide.

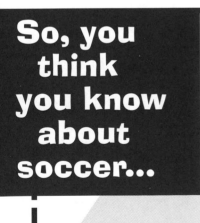

**So, you think you know about soccer...**

How much distance does an average player cover *with the ball* during an average 90-minute match?

A.  200 yards
B.  1,000 yards
C.  1 mile
D.  2 miles

Answer: A. (Not as much as you thought, huh?)

**GOAL AREA (also called "Goal box"):** Area, 6 yards long and 18 yards wide, inside penalty area; goal kicks are taken from anywhere inside goal area.

**GOAL HANGER:** Player who hangs around the goal mouth, hoping to get a pass and score. Goal hangers seldom play defense; hence, term is usually derogatory. Action of goal hangers is "goal hanging."

**GOALKEEPER (also called "Goalie" and "Keeper"):** Sole player on field allowed to use his or her hands (only within penalty area). Main job is to keep ball out of goal; also important is initiating attack after save or back pass. In recent years, rule changes have resulted in goalkeepers roaming far outside box, playing much more offensive roles.

**GOAL KICK:** When offensive team takes a shot that misses goal but crosses goal line completely, defensive team is awarded goal kick. They put the ball in play from anywhere within goal area

(smaller area inside penalty area). Ball must leave penalty area before it can be touched by another player.

**GOAL LINE:** Boundary line extending from one side of field to another; also called "end line." Ball must be entirely over goal line to be out of bounds; if it is shot between goal posts, must go entirely over goal line to count as a goal. Goal line must be no shorter than 50 yards wide, no longer than 100 yards wide.

**GOALMOUTH:** Area in front of soccer goal.

**GOALPOST:** The two 8-foot-high vertical posts that form outer edges of goal. Not to be confused with "crossbar" (horizontal bar across top). Goalposts were originally made from wood; now, most are constructed of aluminum.

**GOAL SIDE:** Term referring to positioning of a defender. Being "goal side" means positioning oneself between the attacker with the ball, and the goal, so that attacker must go directly through or around defender to score.

**GOLDEN GOAL:** Goal scored in overtime that immediately ends match. Formerly called "sudden death."

**GOTHIA CUP:** Youth tournament held every year in Gothenburg, Sweden; with over 1,000 teams, considered the world's largest youth tournament.

**GREER, DON:** Longtime U.S. youth soccer leader; elected to U.S. National Soccer Hall of Fame, 1985.

**GREER CUP (DON GREER CUP):** Snickers National Youth Championship for boys' U-17 teams.

**GREGG, LAUREN:** Assistant coach, U.S. national women's team; head coach, U-21 women's team. In 1989, became first woman to serve as assistant coach for any U.S. national team. Former head coach, University of Virginia; in 1990 became only woman named NSCAA Coach of the Year. First woman to lead a

team to NCAA Division I Final Four. All-American player at University of North Carolina.

**GRIDS:** Square or rectangular areas used for training; can be marked with cones or lines.

**GULATI, SUNIL:** For many years, one of the most powerful "behind-scenes" men in American soccer; currently managing director of U.S. Soccer's Project 2010. As second-in-command at Major League Soccer through 1998, was responsible for signing many international stars. Also served as an assistant professor of economics at Columbia University, and worked at the World Bank.

**GULLIT, RUUD:** Dutch star of late 1980s and '90s. Known for intelligence and distinctive dreadlocks. After starring for PSV Eindhoven and AC Milan, knee problems ended his career.

# H

utes long. After halftime, two teams switch ends of field.

**HALF VOLLEY:** Like a volley, except ball is struck as soon as it hits the ground, and begins rising back up.

**HALFWAY LINE:** Line running across field, designating the center. A player cannot be offside if he is on his defensive side of the field. Also called "midfield stripe."

**HADJI, MUSTAPHA:** Moroccan national team star. Flashy dribbler, dangerous scorer; key goals include brilliant strike against Norway at 1998 World Cup, and bicycle kick against Egypt in 1998 African Nations' Cup. Named 1998 African Footballer of Year. Current club team: Deportiva la Corua (Spain).

**HAGI, GEORGHE:** Romanian national team star. Current club team: Galatasaray SK (Turkey).

**HALFTIME:** Intermission of a soccer game; usually 5–10 min-

**HAMM, MIA:** U.S. national team star, whose combination of strength, grace, acceleration, and goal-scoring ability make her perhaps the world's best female player; tremendous role model for younger players. At 15 became youngest player ever on U.S. national team, male or female. Played in 1991, '95, and '99 Women's World Cups; made penalty kick to help the United States win

**FOOTNOTE:**
Mia Hamm was the youngest player ever to appear for the U.S. women's national team (15 years, 140 days).

'99 title. In 1999, her 108th international goal, in 3–0 win over Brazil, beat career record for men and women (previous holder: Elisabetta Vignotta of Italy). Has her own signature Barbie Doll, has a building named after her at Nike headquarters, was voted one of 50 most beautiful people by *People* magazine, is author of book *Go for the Goal: A Champion's Guide to Winning in Soccer and Life,* and organized the Mia Hamm Foundation, which supports research into bone marrow disease and encourages development of young female athletes.

**HAND BALL:** An infraction committed by any field player anywhere on the field, and by any goalkeeper outside penalty area. Players will be called for a hand ball unless, in judgment of referee, contact was both unintentional and incidental (not resulting in a change of direction of ball). When a team commits such a foul, opposing team receives a direct kick. If hand ball occurs in penalty area, opposing team receives a penalty kick.

**HARKES, JOHN:** Longtime captain of U.S. national team; dropped from squad by coach Steve Sampson just weeks before 1998 World Cup, for alleged training violations and leadership failures. Rejoined national team 15 months later, in 1999. Wrote book, *Captain for Life and Other Temporary Assignments,* in

Mia Hamm

1999. As captain and midfielder, helped D.C. United win Major League Soccer championships (1996, '97). Also played in England for West Ham United, Derby County, and Sheffield Wednesday, where he became the first American to score a goal in the prestigious Coca-Cola League Cup Final at Wembley, and the first American to play in UEFA Cup. In 1990, his 35-yard rocket was named England's Goal of Year. Youth soccer teammate of Tab Ramos. Current MLS team: New England Revolution.

**HAT TRICK:** Feat of scoring three goals in one game (originally, referred to feat of scoring three *consecutive* goals in a game).

**HAVELANGE, JOAO:** Six-term president of FIFA (1974–98); credited with bringing soccer into the modern era, and advancing women's soccer worldwide. Native of Brazil.

**HEADING:** Clearing or shooting the ball with one's head. Proper heading technique involves arching torso back, then "punching through" ball as it meets hairline. Headed balls are called "headers."

**HEINRICHS, APRIL:** Former U.S. national team assistant coach; currently U-16 women's national team head coach, and head coach at University of Virginia. Pioneer on U.S. women's national team; in 1988, first female player inducted into U.S. National Soccer Hall of Fame. Captain of 1991 U.S. team, which won first Women's World Cup; finished

## FUN SOCCER FACTS

Mia Hamm's husband, Christian Corry, is a U.S. Marine Corps pilot. President Clinton arranged for him to be granted special leave to see the 1999 Women's World Cup finals.

career with 38 goals in 47 games. Named U.S. Soccer Female Athlete of Year, 1986 and '89; voted Female Player of the '80s by *Soccer America* magazine; three-time All-American at University of North Carolina, where she led Tar Heels to three NCAA championships. Elected to U.S. National Soccer Hall of Fame, 1998.

**HEJDUK, FRANKIE:** U.S. national team player; one of few bright spots at 1998 World Cup. Fast striker who creates many chances from flank; long flowing hair and "surfer" persona make him a crowd favorite. Current club team: Bayer Leverkusen (Germany).

**HENRY, THIERRY:** French starter and star, 1998 World Cup.

**HERMANN TROPHY:** Awarded annually to top NCAA Division I male and female soccer players in the United States, based on voting by Division I coaches and selected sportswriters. Named after Robert Hermann, founding chairman of North American Soccer League. Equivalent of college football's Heisman Trophy.

**HEYSEL:** Stadium in Brussels; site of 1985 disaster where 39 people died and 400 spectators were injured when wall collapsed during rioting started by English fans prior to European Cup final between Liverpool and Juventus. Tragedy captured on live TV. As a result, English teams were banned from European competition.

**HILL, LAURIE:** Star of Mexico's women's national team; an American citizen, she is eligible for Mexico's team because her mother is a native of Mexico City. Three-time All-American at the University of California, Santa Barbara.

**HILLSBOROUGH:** Stadium in Sheffield, England; site of Britain's worst sports disaster, where 95 Liverpool fans were crushed to death and almost 200 injured before F.A. Cup semifinal against Nottingham Forest, when surging crowd forced others into security fences. Tragedy led to dismantling of such fences, and requirements for all-seat stadiums.

**HOFFMAN, JAY:** Assistant coach, U.S. national women's team; previously, head coach, U.S. men's U-20 national team. Since 1992, a U.S. Soccer coaching coordinator.

**"HOLD!":** Signal from one player to a teammate that he or she should hold onto the ball, wait for support, and not try to go forward too quickly.

**HOLDING:** Illegally using hands to restrain opponent. Holding foul results in a direct kick by opposing team.

**HOLLAND:** Two-time World Cup runners-up: 1974 (2–1 to West Germany, after scoring in first minute on penalty kick); 1978 (3–1 to Argentina in overtime). Known for "total soccer," in which players interchange roles constantly. Nickname: "Clockwork Orange." Retirement of key players led to slippage in the 1980s, but Holland surged again in the '90s. Charter member of FIFA (1904).

**HOOLIGANS:** Soccer fans more interested in creating disturbances than watching the game. Although hooligans are generally thought to be English, they can actually come from any country.

**HOOPER, CHARMAINE:** Top player and all-time leading scorer on Canadian women's national team; free kick helped FIFA World All-Stars beat the United States in 1999. Attacking midfielder; two-time All-American at North Carolina State University.

**HOSPITAL PASS:** Weak pass; so called because it allows an opponent to race through, tackle hard, and send the teammate receiving ball to the hospital. Also called "hospital ball" or "buddy pass."

**HOWE, BOBBY:** Director of coaching, U.S. Soccer Federation.

# FUN SOCCER FACTS

John Harkes's wife, Cindi, is a former soccer standout at the University of Virginia, and trained with the U.S. women's national team in 1994.

Frankie Hejduk proposed marriage to his wife, Kim, in knee-deep water off San Diego, while holding a surfboard.

**HUNGARY:** One of the world's top teams in the 1950s; World Cup runners-up to Italy in 1938 World Cup, again in 1954 to West Germany (after losing only one match in previous five years). In 1953, first non-British team to beat England at home, by amazing 6–3 score. Considered (with Holland of 1970s) one of two best teams never to win the World Cup.

**HUNT, LAMAR:** For 30 years, a leader in American professional soccer. Oil businessman with inherited wealth; invested in Dallas Tornado of fledgling North American Soccer League in 1968, and provided stability to the league through 1981, despite losing millions of dollars. Original investor-operator in Major League Soccer in 1996, with investment of many millions of dollars.

Developed Columbus Crew Stadium, first soccer-specific major facility in the United States. Member of U.S. National Soccer Hall of Fame and, as a founder of American Football League, of Football Hall of Fame as well.

**HURST, GEOFF:** English star; in 1966 scored first-ever hat trick in World Cup history. His second goal, during overtime in the final against Germany, was one of the most controversial ever, when slammed off underside of goalpost. To this day no one knows which side of the line the ball bounced on, but the referee ruled it a goal. England went on to defeat West Germany, 4–2.

## So, you think you know about soccer...

Which is the only World Cup champion not to defend its title?

A. Uruguay
B. West Germany
C. Brazil
D. Italy

Answer: A. In 1934, Uruguay, the first champion, refused to travel to Italy. They were mad at European teams' refusal to come to Uruguay in 1930, and were plagued by players' strikes as well.

**I**

**INDIANA UNIVERSITY:**
One of the most successful
men's college teams of all
time; between 1982 and '98,
won four NCAA Division I
championships.

**INDIRECT KICK:** A free
kick awarded for a foul that
does not involve physical
contact (for example, dangerous play, obstruction, delay
of game, or unsportsmanlike
conduct). An indirect kick
may not go into goal until at
least one other player (on
either team) has touched the
ball after it is initially kicked.
Defenders must remain at
least 10 yards away before

ball is kicked. An indirect
kick foul awarded inside
penalty area is treated just
like another indirect kick;
however, if foul occurs less
than 10 yards from the goal
line, defenders may line up
on goal line.

**INDOOR SOCCER:** A great
debate has raged for years as
to whether indoor soccer is
simply an indoor version of
the outdoor game, or a sepa-
rate sport entirely. For years,
indoor soccer was simply a
way to train indoors, using
existing lines on basketball
courts or gym floors. However, when indoor U.S.
leagues proliferated in the
1970s and '80s, they added
"dasher boards" off of which
the ball could be played,
much like ice hockey. Some
indoor soccer leagues have
added other rules, such as
prohibiting the ball from
being played forward over a
certain number of lines.

**INFRACTION:** See "foul."

**IN-HOUSE SOCCER:** Also
called recreational soccer;
least competitive level of

soccer. Called "in-house" because all teams come under the control of one club or youth sports organization.

**INJURY TIME:** Time added on by referee, at end of each half, due to injuries or other long stoppages of play. Referee is the timekeeper, and adds injury time at own discretion.

**INSIDE OF THE FOOT PASS:** Pass using inside of the foot; best for short, accurate passes.

**INSTEP:** Part of the foot near laces; used for kicking ("driving" the ball). Commonly confused with "inside of the foot."

**INSWINGER:** Corner kick that curves inward, toward the goal.

**INTERAMERICAN CUP:** Tournament between champions of CONCACAF (North and Central America, and the Caribbean) and CONMEBOL (South America).

**INTERNATIONAL SOCCER LEAGUE:** U.S. league, begun in 1960; comprised of top European and South American teams, as an attempt to test support of American fans for high-level league.

**INTERVAL:** English term for "halftime."

**ITALY:** From the 1930s on, one of the world's top teams; professional league is considered best in the world. Until 1980s, teams characterized by an emphasis on defense, with bursts of counterattacks. Italy hosted 1934 and '90 World Cups; won '34 Cup, 2–1 over Czechoslovakia in overtime. Defended World Cup championship successfully in 1938, with 4–2 victory over Hungary in France. Won again in 1982 in Spain, with 3–1 victory over West Germany. Hosted World Cup in 1990 (winner: West Germany). Two-time runners-up: 1970 (4–1 to Brazil), 1994 (on penalty kicks to Italy, following 0–0 draw).

Championship. Full national team is first from outside Western Hemisphere to play in Copa America (1999).

**JEFFREY, BILL:** Legendary coach at Pennsylvania State University; elected to U.S. National Soccer Hall of Fame, 1951.

**JERSEY:** A soccer shirt.

**J-LEAGUE:** Professional league in Japan; known in the mid-'90s for excessive salaries paid to foreign players. Economic problems have since curtailed the high-flying league.

**JOHANSSON, LENNART:** President of UEFA (second-most powerful position in FIFA); defeated in campaign for FIFA presidency, 1998.

**JOHN, ELTON:** Chairman of Watford (English Premier League); also known as a singer/piano player.

**JOHN, STERN:** MLS scoring sensation with Columbus Crew.

**JACQUET, AIME:** Coach of France's World Cup–winning team in 1998; resigned after finals to accept administrative role with French soccer federation.

**JAIRZINHO:** Brazilian star of the 1960s and early '70s. In 1970 World Cup, scored in every round to help lead Brazil to title.

**JAPAN:** Although not a recognized soccer power, Japan will cohost 2002 World Cup with South Korea. Women's and youth teams are particularly strong; U-20 team was runner-up in 1999 World

**JOHNSTON, MO:** Former Celtic star from Glasgow who, in 1989, became first Catholic since World War I to sign with archrival Rangers. Current MLS team: Kansas City Wizards.

**JONES, COBI:** One of only two U.S. national team players to play every game of 1994 and '98 World Cups; youngest male player in the world to reach 100 international appearances. Fast midfielder; long dreadlocks make him instantly recognizable. Current MLS team: Los Angeles Galaxy.

## FUN SOCCER FACTS

The first soccer shirts were made of thick wool, but cotton soon proved to be cheaper and more practical. Later, synthetics allowed maximum ventilation. For many years, however, collar fronts featured buttons, laces, or even zippers.

**JULES RIMET TROPHY:** Official name of World Cup trophy, beginning in 1950; named for president of FIFA and French federations during the 1920s. After winning third World Cup in 1970, Brazil retired Jules Rimet trophy.

**FOOTNOTE:**
In 1994, Cobi Jones made a guest appearance on *Beverly Hills 90210.*

**JUGGLING:** Keeping ball off ground using any part of body. Very effective in developing good touch on ball.

**JUVENTUS:** Turin, Italy, team founded in 1897; called "Italy's team," because of many national team players they have produced (six on 1982's World Cup winners). In the 1990s, stars included Roberto Baggio and Gianluca Vialli. In Italian, "juventus" means "youth."

**K**

will save a ball, and all other defenders should move out.

**KELLER, KASEY:** Considered one of the top goalkeepers in the world; turned in what has been called best goalkeeping performance ever in the United States in 1–0 shutout of Brazil in 1998 (Romario: "It was an honor to be on the field with him"). Has started twice as many professional games as any other U.S. player in Europe. Current club team: Rayo Vallecano (Spain).

**KANSAS CITY WIZARDS:** Charter member of Major League Soccer (MLS).

**KEEGAN, KEVIN:** Former Liverpool and Hamburg star, and captain of the English national team; named coach of English national team, 1999.

FOOTNOTE: Kasey Keller grew up on an egg farm in Lacey, Washington.

**KEEPAWAY:** Training game used to develop touch, possession, decision-making, and defensive positioning.

**KEEPER:** See "goalkeeper" for description of position. When shouted as a command, "Keeper!" means goalkeeper

**KEMPES, MARIO:** Argentine national team star of the 1970s; scored two goals in 1978 World Cup final 3–1 win over Holland. Known for massive legs.

**KEOUGH, HARRY:** Legendary coach, Saint Louis University; elected to U.S.

National Soccer Hall of Fame, 1976.

**KICKER:** German magazine; one of the world's leading soccer publications.

**KICKOFF:** Each half- and overtime period of a game begins with a kickoff; which team kicks off when is determined during pregame meeting with referees and captains, via coin flip. A kickoff also restarts play following each goal; team that was scored upon kicks off. During kickoff, opponents must stand outside center circle (radius: 10 yards).

**KIT:** Term for an entire soccer uniform, from jersey to shoes.

**KLEINAITIS, ALFRED:** Veteran soccer referee; currently director of officials for U.S. Soccer. Elected to U.S. National Soccer Hall of Fame, 1995.

**KLINSMANN, JUERGEN:** One of Germany's best players ever. Captained national team, and played on squad for 11 years. Helped win World Cup in 1990.

**KLUIVERT, PATRICK:** Dutch national team star; as teenager, scored game-winning goal for Ajax in 1996 UEFA Champion's League final. Dangerous in the air, with excellent first touch. Current club team: Barcelona (Spain).

# THE WORLD'S GREATEST GAMES
# 1970

**World Cup, first round: Brazil 1, England 0 (includes Gordon Banks's spectacular first–half save on Pele; only goal scored in second half by Jairzinho)**

**KNOCKOUT TOURNA-MENT:** Tournament in which one loss eliminates a team; also called "single elimination."

**KREIS, JASON:** College star at Duke University; current star for MLS Dallas Burn.

Juergen Klinsmann

# L

**LALAS, ALEXI:** Emerged from 1994 World Cup as one of the world's most recognizable players; long red hair, goatee, and crushing defense all helped contribute to his selection for All-World Cup team. First American-born and raised player to compete in Italy's Serie A. Also known as rock guitarist and singer. Current MLS team: Kansas City Wizards.

**LASSITER, ROY:** Striker; boasts one of the highest goals-per-minutes-played averages on U.S. national team. One of first American stars in MLS. Current MLS team: D.C. United.

**LAUDRUP, BRIAN:** Danish midfielder. Burst on international scene at age 18; scored 21 goals in 81 international matches, and helped Denmark win European championship in 1992. Re-tired in 1999, after stints with Broendby, Bayer Uerdingen, Bayern Munich, Fiorentina, AC Milan, Glas-gow Rangers, Chelsea, and FC Copenhagen. Older brother Michael also a Danish and international star.

**LAWS OF THE GAME:** Official name for "Rules of Soccer." There are 17 Laws; 18th is "advantage," or common sense: If a team that was fouled against will be penalized by a referee stopping play, official should allow play to continue.

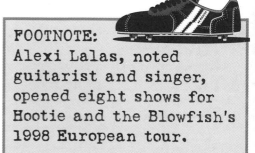

FOOTNOTE:
Alexi Lalas, noted guitarist and singer, opened eight shows for Hootie and the Blowfish's 1998 European tour.

**"LAY IT!":** Command for a player to send a pass on the ground to an onrushing teammate.

**"LET IT RUN!":** Signal from one player to a teammate about to receive ball that he or she does not need to control it, but can turn and let it "run" (roll) forward, either because the teammate has plenty of space, or because another teammate farther upfield should receive it.

**LEWIS, EDDIE:** Up-and-coming U.S. national team star; made his name with current MLS team, San Jose Clash.

**LEWIS, VIRGIL:** Chairman, U.S. Youth Soccer Association; attorney.

**LIBERIA:** Strong African team, thanks to presence of George Weah, first African to be named FIFA Player of the Year.

**LIBERO:** See "sweeper."

**LIBERTADORES CUP:** South American champions' cup.

**LICENSE (Coaching):** Around the world, various professional organizations offer coaching licenses (also

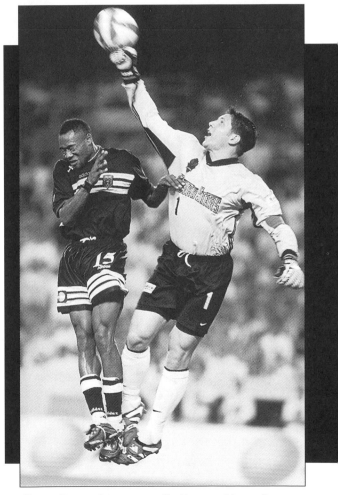

**Roy Lassiter and Tony Merola**

called "badges") to certify that recipient has passed a coaching course. In the United States, courses range from elementary (nine hours) to rigorous (week-long residence camps, with written and practical tests of theory and skill). Two major U.S. licensing organizations: U.S. Soccer and National Soccer Coaches Association of America.

**LILLY, KRISTINE:** U.S. women's national team star who played in 1991, '95, and '99 Women's World Cups; scored penalty kick to help the United States win '99 title, after clearing certain goal off line near the end of regulation time. After Mia Hamm, considered the best all-around player in women's soccer. Holds world record for caps (appearances with a national team); third leading scorer in U.S. women's soccer history. In 1998, set U.S. record for consecutive games started (62). Very hard-working left-footed, left-side midfielder who moves forward aggressively; role model for young players everywhere.

**LIMITED SUBSTITUTION:** Policy of allowing only a set number of substitutions; once a player has left a match, he may not reenter. At younger levels of soccer, there is unlimited substitution.

**LINEKER, GARY:** Star English striker of the 1980s; second-leading scorer in English history.

**LINESMEN:** Also called "assistant referees." One on each side of field; in charge of spotting offside offenses and other infractions that central referee may miss. Also determine out of bounds, and help substitutes enter the game.

**LIVERPOOL:** One of England's most famous soccer clubs; founded in 1892. Winner of many titles, but also known for two disasters. In 1985, 39 people died and more than 400 were injured when fans rioted during match against Juventus in Brussels. Four years later, in Britain's worst sports disaster, 95 Liverpool fans were crushed to death and nearly

200 hurt before F.A. Cup semifinal in Sheffield.

**LOGAN, DOUG:** First commissioner of Major League Soccer (1995–99).

**LONG BALL:** A long pass through the air, either forward or from one side of the field to the other.

**LOS ANGELES GALAXY:** Charter member of Major League Soccer (MLS); known for excellent regular season records, but inability to produce in postseason playoffs.

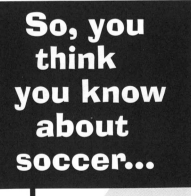

## FUN SOCCER FACTS

Tony Meola tried out as a place kicker with the New York Jets after the 1994 World Cup. The next year he appeared in the off-Broadway comedy, "Tony and Tina's Wedding."

## So, you think you know about soccer...

Question: How much distance does an average soccer player cover during an average 90-minute match?

A. 1½ miles
B. 7 miles
C. 10 miles
D. 15 miles

Answer: B. (Referees cover a lot more! And goalkeepers cover 2½ miles, mostly moving around their box.)

# M

**McGUIRE CUP (JAMES P. McGUIRE CUP):** Snickers National Youth Championship for boys' U-19 teams; most prestigious of all national youth trophies, dating back to 1935.

**McKEON, MATT:** Defensive midfield star with MLS team Colorado Rapids.

**MACMILLAN, SHANNON:** Member of U.S. national women's team; scored "golden goal" against Norway that put the United States into the 1996 Olympic final. In 1995, at the University of Portland, won both the Hermann Trophy and Missouri Athletic Club Award, and was named Soccer America Female Player of Year.

**McBRIDE, BRIAN:** One of few bright spots on U.S. national team during World Cup 1998; particularly dangerous in air. Scored 1998 MLS Goal of the Year. Current MLS team: Columbus Crew.

**MACCABI GAMES:** Worldwide event for Jewish athletes; adult games held every four years, youth games every two years. Contact information: Maccabi USA/Sports for Israel; tel.: (215) 561-6900; fax: (215) 561-5470.

**"MAGIC MAGYARS":** Nickname of the great Hungarian national teams of 1950s.

**MAISONNEUVE, BRIAN:** Rising star on U.S. national team; one of first two college players to sign MLS contract.

Current MLS team: Columbus Crew.

**MAJOR INDOOR SOCCER LEAGUE (MISL):** Professional indoor soccer league; debuted in 1978 with six franchises. Folded in 1992.

**MAJOR LEAGUE SOCCER (MLS):** Top professional league in the United States; 10 teams competed in first season, 1996, with two more added in 1998. Aspires to be "fifth major professional sports league" in the United States; with static attendance, low-budget television contract, and poor media coverage, it has a long way to go. League allocates players to teams; MLS also has a limit on foreign players, and salary cap. Contact information: 110 E. 42nd St., 10th Floor, New York, NY 10017; tel.: (212) 450-1200; fax: (212) 450-1300; Web site: www.mlsnet.com.

**MALDINI, PAULO:** Italian national team star; one of the world's top defenders. Won UEFA Champions' League, Italian League, and Italian Cup titles before 23rd birthday. Current club team: AC Milan (Italy).

**MANAGER:** In the United States, refers to a father or mother who handles a youth soccer team's administrative details. In England, "manager" is what Americans refer to as "coach."

**MANCHESTER UNITED:** One of the world's oldest and most popular clubs; founded in 1878. In 1958, several months after losing eight players in airplane crash, reached semifinals of European Cup. Ten years later, "Man U." won European championship with team that included three crash survivors, including coach Matt Busby. In 1999, it became the first English team to win "triple crown"—league, F.A. Cup, and continental championship—in one season. In incredible final match against Bayern Munich, Teddy Sheringham and Ole Gunnar Solskjaer came off bench to score injury time goals off corner kicks to key come-from-behind, 2–1 victory. In the '90s, won five league titles, four cup crowns, and three "doubles" in six years; considered the richest club in world (well ahead of Barcelona). Old Trafford stadium known as "The Theatre of Dreams."

**MAN DOWN:** Team that has had player ejected, or lost one to injury, is said to be playing a "man down." Women's teams use same terminology. According to FIFA rules, team may lose as many as four players before a match is abandoned.

**"MAN ON!":** Signal from one player to teammate about to receive pass that he or she is being guarded (marked) closely, and should not attempt to turn or move too quickly with the ball. Generic expression; used by females as well as males.

**MAN-TO-MAN MARK-ING:** Defensive tactic in which each defender covers, or "marks," one attacker. Term is used even for female players.

**MARACANA:** Located in Rio de Janeiro; home field of Fluminense. One of the world's most famous stadiums, with room for over 150,000 spectators; many Brazilian national team games are played at Maracana. Built for World Cup in 1950; more than 200,000 spectators squeezed in for final match between Brazil and Uruguay. Underwent extensive renovation in the late '90s.

**MARADONA, DIEGO:** Best soccer player in the world during the 1980s; also one of

Maradona Lifts the World Cup Trophy, Mexico 1986

the most controversial. Captained World Cup–winning Argentina team in 1986, and was unanimous choice as Player of the Tournament, but scored one goal by punching ball into the net ("Hand of God"). Was also known for rough style of play, unsportsmanlike attitude, and drug problems.

**FUN SOCCER FACTS**

The U.S. men's national team's greatest goal-scoring output came in a 1993 win over the Cayman Islands: 8-1. The worst loss came in 1948: an 11-0 defeat by Norway.

**MARCOS, FRANCISCO:** Founder, current commissioner/president, United Soccer Leagues; longtime soccer administrator.

**MARKING:** Another word for "defending." One player "marks" another; the player he or she is marking becomes the "mark."

**"MARK UP!":** Call from goalkeeper or defender, urging teammates to move upfield and begin marking opponents.

**MARSEILLE:** First French club to win European Cup (1993); title was revoked in game-fixing scandal. Millionaire owner Bernard Tapie had invested millions in pursuit of championship.

**MASOTTO CUP (PATRICIA MASOTTO CUP):** Snickers National Youth Championship for girls' U-16 teams.

**MATCH:** A soccer game. Official "match" is 90 minutes long (shorter for younger ages).

**MATTHAEUS, LOTHAR:** German international star; Bayern Munich sweeper and captain of West Germany's 1990 World Cup–winning team; voted Player of the Tournament.

**MATTHEWS, SIR STANLEY:** First great English player after World War I; knighted by Queen for honor he brought to country. Right-winger with great dribbling skills, played in England's top division for an incredible 33 years, until age 50—and never once was ejected.

**MENOTTI, CESAR:** Coach of Argentina's 1978 World Cup–winning team.

**MEOLA, TONY:** Most international appearances (87) of any goalkeeper in U.S. history; played in 1990 and '94 World Cups. Rejuvenated career with MLS. Current MLS team: Kansas City Wizards.

**MESSING, SHEP:** First U.S. national team goalkeeping star (1970s).

**MEXICO:** Longtime undisputed champion of CONCA-CAF (North American, Central American, and Caribbean) region; supremacy recently challenged by the United States. Mexico–U.S. rivalry is one of the biggest in world soccer. Mexico hosted 1970 World Cup, first non-European or South American nation to do so (winner: Brazil). In 1986, became the first country to host two World Cups, when Colombia withdrew as host nation because of domestic

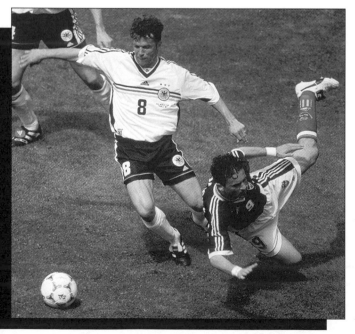

Lothar Matthaeus

problems (winner: Argentina).

**MIAMI FUSION:** Expansion team; joined Major League Soccer (MLS) in 1998.

**MICHELS, RINUS:** Dutch coach; developed "total soccer" system (in which players constantly interchange positions), first with Ajax, later with national team.

**MIDFIELD:** Central part of field. Also refers to all midfielders collectively.

Tony Meola

**MIDFIELDER:** Position in the middle of field. Midfielders act as links between defenders and strikers, must be adept at both offense and defense. Good midfielders direct pace and direction of the attack. Position includes both outside (flank) and central midfielders.

**MIDFIELD STRIPE:** Line running across field, desig-nating center. A player cannot be offside if he is on his defensive side of field. Also called "midfield line" and "halfway line."

**MILBRETT, TIFFENY:** U.S. women's national team player; 5'2" forward adept at weaving through defenders. Led the United States with three goals at 1995 World Cup; scored game-winner in 1996 Olympic finals.

**MILLA, ROGER:** Longtime Cameroon star; twice voted African Footballer of Year, 14 years apart (1976 and '90). Played most of career in France. Known for exotic celebrations after scoring goals.

**MILLER, AL:** Veteran U.S. college and youth coach; elected to U.S. National

> **FOOTNOTE:**
> Joe-Max Moore grew up hanging around the Tulsa Roughnecks of the North American Soccer League. His father owned the team.

Soccer Hall of Fame, 1995.

**MILUTINOVIC, BORA:** Known universally by first name; served as U.S. national team coach from 1991 to '95, including World Cup 1994, which the United States hosted. Serbia-born, multilingual Bora enjoyed earlier success as national team coach of Mexico and Costa Rica; served as head coach of Nigeria at 1998 World Cup. Currently coach of MLS team

New York/New Jersey MetroStars.

**MISSOURI ATHLETIC CLUB (MAC) AWARD:** Presented annually to top collegiate male and female players of the year; recipients must be American citizens. Voted on by college coaches.

**MIXER:** English expression meaning "penalty box." "Put it in the mixer!" means "send a long pass into the box!"

**MLS CUP:** Major League Soccer (MLS) championship game. D.C. United won first two Cups; expansion team Chicago Fire captured 1998 title.

**"MOLDEDS":** Nickname given to soccer shoes made of molded rubber.

**MOORE, BOBBY:** Captain of England's 1966 World Cup championship team; known for calm demeanor. Later played in North American Soccer League.

**MOORE, JOE-MAX:** One of the leading scorers in U.S.

national team history; member of 1994 and '98 World Cup teams. Free kick specialist. Current MLS team: New England Revolution.

**MORACE, CAROLINA:** Italian female player who retired with 105 goals, then the second most in soccer history. Currently, first woman to coach men's team in Italy (amateur club Vis Aurelia).

**MOUTH GUARD:** Sometimes used by players after jaw or dental injury; disliked by most, for interference with verbal communication.

**MULLER, GERD:** German star of the 1970s; nicknamed "Der Bomber" for wicked shot. Scored 68 goals in 62 international matches, including winning goal in 2–1 1974 World Cup final against Holland. Had record 365 goals in Bundesliga.

**MURRAY, BRUCE:** U.S. national team standout, 1985–93. Forward, scored 21 goals in 86 international matches.

**MURRAY, MITCH:** Head coach, U.S. men's U-18 national team.

**MYERNICK, GLENN:** Former U.S. national team assistant coach; one of the first American-born players to make a mark as coach. Took MLS team Colorado Rapids to championship in 1997. Nickname: "Mooch."

## THE WORLD'S GREATEST GAMES
# 1986

**World Cup final: Argentina 3, West Germany 2 (West Germans rally from 2–0 deficit, only to lose on goal by Burruchaga)**

**NACIONAL:** Based in Montevideo, traditionally one of Uruguay's top clubs. Celebrated 100th anniversary in 1999, but facing harsh economic conditions. One of only three teams to win three Intercontinental Cup titles.

**NATIONAL ASSOCIATION OF INTERCOLLEGIATE ATHLETICS (NAIA):** Governing body for collegiate soccer not organized by NCAA. Contact information: tel.: (918) 494-8828; fax: (918) 494-8841.

**NATIONAL COLLEGIATE ATHLETIC ASSOCIATION (NCAA):** Governing body for most collegiate soccer in the United States (other major body is NAIA; see above). NCAA organizes national tournaments each fall for three men's divisions (I, II, and III), and two women's divisions (I and II). First tournament: 1959. Contact information: tel.: (913) 339-1906; fax: (913) 339-1950.

**NATIONAL INTERCOLLEGIATE SOCCER OFFICIALS ASSOCIATION:** Governing body for college soccer officials. Contact information: tel.: (407) 862-3305; fax: (407) 862-8545.

**NATIONAL PROFESSIONAL SOCCER LEAGUE (NPSL):** Indoor league; season runs October through April. Founded 1984 as American Indoor Soccer Association; became NPSL in 1990. Contact information: 115 Dewalt Ave. NW, 5th Floor, Canton, OH 44720; tel.: (216) 455-4625; fax: (216) 455-3885. League with same name organized in 1967; merged at end of year with United Soccer Association, to form North American Soccer League.

**NATIONAL SOCCER COACHES ASSOCIATION OF AMERICA (NSCAA):** Founded in 1941 by 10 coaches; today boasts over 10,000 members, and calls itself largest coaching organization of any kind in the world. Members range from novice youth coaches to college. Publishes bimonthly *Soccer Journal,* and offers coaching courses. Contact information: 6700 Squibb Rd., Suite 215, Fairway, KS 66202; tel.: 1-800- 458-0678; fax: (913) 362-3439.

**NATIONAL SOCCER HALL OF FAME:** Formed in 1950; since 1979, located in Oneonta, New York. Contains offices, museum store, library, archive area, lecture hall, memorabilia, interactive exhibits. Plans underway for stadium, additional fields, and indoor arena. Over 220 men and women have been selected to the Hall of Fame based on outstanding contributions to soccer, on and off the field. Contact information: 5–11 Ford Ave., Oneonta, NY 13820; tel.: (607) 432-3351; fax: (607) 432-8429; Web site: www.soccerhall.org.

**NATIONAL TEAM:** Any team representing a nation in international competition. "Full" national team is men's or women's adult team, but may be other national teams as well. In the United States, U.S. Soccer organizes and manages nine national teams: men's full national team, U-23 (Olympic), U-20, U-18, U-17, and futsal (five-a-side); women's full national team, U-21, and U-18. Men's and women's U-16 and U-14 teams are considered "developmental."

**NEAR POST:** Goalpost closest to the shooter or defender.

**NEESKENS, JOHAN:** Aggressive midfield star of great Dutch teams of the 1970s; also played with New York Cosmos of North American Soccer League.

**NET:** Attached to goalposts to prevent arguments over whether the ball actually went into the goal (or curved around from outside). For that reason, nets should be secured in back, and on side, with stakes. Most nets are made of nylon.

**NETHERLANDS, THE:** See Holland.

**NETZER, GUNTER:** West German midfielder star in the 1960s and '70s; worked well with Franz Beckenbauer.

**NEW ENGLAND REVOLU-TION:** Charter member of Major League Soccer (MLS); seldom successful on field, but league leader in attendance. Hosted the inaugural Soccer Bowl championship in 1996; drew 50,000 fans in monsoon.

**NEWMAN, RON:** Veteran outdoor and indoor coach; 30-year career in the United States spanned both North American Soccer League and Major League Soccer.

**NEW YORK/NEW JERSEY METROSTARS:** Charter member of Major League Soccer (MLS); playing at Giants Stadium and expected to pick up mantle of Cosmos of failed North American Soccer League; but for its first three years, one of the weakest teams in MLS. Hired five coaches in first four years.

**NIGERIA:** Leading African nation; teams have won several FIFA youth championships, though disputes have arisen regarding overage players. Disappointment in major

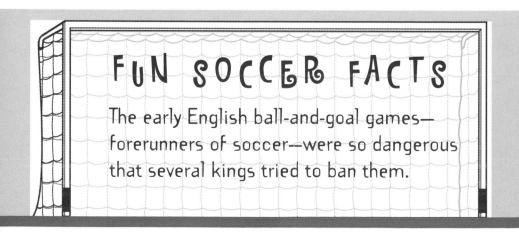

# FUN SOCCER FACTS

The early English ball-and-goal games— forerunners of soccer—were so dangerous that several kings tried to ban them.

events. Nickname: "Green Eagles."

**NIL:** English term for "zero" (3–0 score is "three–nil").

**NIOTIS CUP (D.J. NIOTIS CUP):** Snickers National Youth Championship for U-16 boys' teams.

**NON-RESULTS ORIENTED COMPETITION:** In recent years, concern has grown that youth soccer programs are too competitive for young players. "Non-results oriented competition" is a way to avoid that. Teams compete in leagues and tournaments, but scores and standings are not officially kept. Emphasis is on skill development and fun, not competition.

**NORTH AMERICAN SOCCER LEAGUE (NASL):** Formed in late 1967, league grew slowly, until New York Cosmos coaxed Pele out of retirement in 1975. League then exploded, as other teams signed foreign stars including Eusebio, Bobby Moore, Rodney Marsh, George Best,

and Johan Cruyff, while Cosmos added the likes of Franz Beckenbauer, Giorgio Chinaglia, and Johan Neeskens. But rapid expansion to two dozen teams, lack of national television contract, and high salaries doomed the league. Folded in 1985.

**NORWAY:** One of the leading women's soccer teams in the world. Lost 1991 Women's World Cup to the United States in China; four years later won championship in Sweden.

**NOU CAMP:** Home stadium of Barcelona; one of the world's most famous soccer stadiums. Hosted World Cup opening game, 1982; Olympic final, 1992. Capacity: 130,000.

**NOWAK, PETER:** Playmaker who helped lead Chicago Fire to MLS title in 1999, in its first year as franchise.

**NUTMEG:** Kicking the ball directly between a defender's legs; highly embarrassing for defender. Used as a verb and noun.

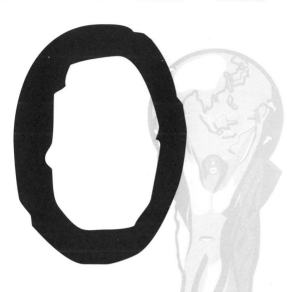

**OBSTRUCTION:** Players are not allowed to obstruct opponents from playing ball, unless it is rolling out of bounds. When obstruction is called, opposing team is awarded an indirect kick.

**OCEANIA FOOTBALL CONFEDERATION (OFC):** One of FIFA's six confederations; includes Australia, New Zealand, and other South Pacific nations. Contact information: tel.: 64-9-525-8161; fax: 64-9-525-8164.

**OFFENSE:** Any time a team possesses the ball, they are on offense. All players on that team are said to be on offense, even if their position is "defense."

**OFFSIDE:** The most difficult rule in soccer to understand and apply correctly. The object of offside is to prevent goal-hanging. One is offside if in one's offensive half of the field, and there are not at least two defensive players between him or her and goal (if the player is *even* with one of the defensive players, he or she is considered onside). Referee will not whistle offside infraction, however, until the ball is passed or shot (in other words, not during a dribble). In addition, referee will not blow whistle if player in offside position is not seeking to gain advantage from that position, or does not interfere with play. When a team is whistled for offside, opposing team restarts play with indirect kick.

**OFFSIDE TRAP:** Defensive maneuver, usually employed by weak defensive teams, in which players move up en masse, attempting to catch attackers offside. Must be executed with precision; easy to beat with long balls, or with players dribbling through defenders.

**"OFF THE BALL":** Any situation occurring outside the immediate area of play.

**O JOGO BONITO:** Brazilian expression for soccer: "The Beautiful Game."

**OKACHA, JAY-JAY:** Nigerian national team star; talented dribbler and play maker who helped lead country to gold medal at 1996 Olympics. Named to 1998 World Cup All-Tournament team. Current club team: Paris Saint-Germain (France).

**OLISEH, SUNDAY:** Nigerian national team star; central defender with dangerous shot. Helped lead country to 1996 Olympic gold medal. In World Cup '98, 35-yard shot ended

Spain's hopes. Current club team: Juventus (Italy).

**OLSEN, BEN:** Rising star on U.S. national and Olympic teams, as well as MLS. Current MLS team: D.C. United.

**OLYMPIC DEVELOPMENT PROGRAM (ODP):** Building blocks of U.S. national team program. Each of 55 U.S. Soccer–affiliated associations runs ODP teams for boys and girls, usually ages 12–19.

Jay-Jay Okacha

Players are selected for their ODP teams (also called "state teams"), and may then progress up ladder to regional and national teams. ODP is called an "identification" program, because it identifies (as well as trains) promising young players.

**OLYMPICS, SUMMER:** For many years, beginning in 1904, soccer competition was a minor affair, limited to amateurs. Recently, the International Olympic Committee has allowed professional players to compete, as long as men are under 23 years old (though each team is allowed three overage players). In 1984 at Los Angeles, men's soccer tournament drew largest crowds of any sport in that year's Olympics. For the United States, most successful Olympic soccer competition took place in 1996, the first year women's teams participated. Playing in front of home crowds, the United States won gold medal. No age restriction in women's Olympic soccer.

**ONEIDAS:** First organized soccer club (Boston) in the United States; undefeated from 1862 to '65. Commemorative monument now stands in Boston Common.

**ONE TOUCH:** Pass made without any "control"; (player receives, then passes or shoots ball without any intervening touches).

**ONE-TWO PASS:** Pass in which one player acts as

## THE WORLD'S GREATEST GAMES
## 1966

World Cup final: England 4, West Germany 2 (West Germans equalized late, 2–2, to send match to overtime; Hurst becomes first player ever to score hat trick in World Cup final) "wall"; after receiving ball, he immediately one-touches it to same player who gave it to him. Also called "wall pass" or "give-and-go."

**ONSIDE:** Opposite of offside. If one is not in an offside position, one is considered onside.

**OPEN SPACE:** Areas of field in which there are few players, thus plenty of room to maneuver.

**ORDER OF MERIT:** Highest honor awarded by FIFA.

**ORTEGA, ARIEL:** Argentine national team star; considered the world's best dribbler and ball handler. Quarterfinal red card for head-butt during World Cup '98 overshadowed his fine play. Current club team: Parma (Italy).

**OSGOOD-SCHLATTER DISEASE:** Growth disease, caused when knee tendon pulls away from growth area; frequently seen in soccer players.

**OUTLET (also called "OUTLET PASS"):** Throw from goalkeeper to teammate; first step in mounting attack after shot on goal.

**OUT OF BOUNDS:** Ball is considered out of bounds (or "out of play") when whole ball crosses whole line. Depending on where ball goes out of bounds, and who touched it last, play can be restarted with a throw-in, goal kick, or corner kick. When a ball goes out of bounds on sideline, it is said to be "out of touch."

**OUTSIDE OF THE FOOT PASS:** Pass struck with outside of foot; usually covers short distance, with ball that bends. Not very accurate.

**OUTSWINGER:** Corner kick that curves outward, away from goal.

**OVERBECK, CARLA:** U.S. women's national team star; captained 1991, '95, and '99 Women's World Cups. Scored penalty kick to help the United States win '99 title. Set record by playing in 63 straight international matches (62 as starter). Defensive anchor. Won four NCAA championships while attending University of North Carolina. As mother of a young son, an inspiration to female athletes.

**OVERLAP:** Form of attack in which player with ball is passed (usually on the outside) by teammate who has just passed ball upfield. "Overlapper" runs by man with ball, then receives quick pass in return. Very difficult to defend against.

**OVERTIME:** Playing extra time, beyond 90 minutes (or other regulation time), in order to determine winner. Overtime can be "golden goal" ("sudden death"), or played to predetermined time, such as 15 or 30 minutes.

**OWEN, MICHAEL:** Burst upon international scene at 1998 World Cup, as 18-year-old striker (youngest player ever to start for England); considered game's next superstar, due to speed and finishing ability. Scored dazzling goal against Argentina after magnificent burst through several defenders; it was named "Goal of the Year." Same year, he was named Premier League Player of the Year. Current club team: Liverpool (England).

**OWN GOAL:** Goal scored unintentionally by member of defending team; usually occurs as deflection, or errant pass back to keeper. An "own goal" is not credited to any member of the scoring team.

# P

awards. Named first-ever winner of Chevrolet/U.S. Soccer Youth Player of Year Award in 1998.

**PARREIRA, CARLOS:** Coach of Brazil's 1994 World Cup–winning team.

**PARRY:** Goalkeeping maneuver to deflect ball away from the goal, or over the top of crossbar.

**PASSARELLA, DANIEL:** Argentine national team star of the 1970s; captain of 1978 World Cup champions. Strong defender, equally adept on offense. Later coached River Plate.

**PASSING:** Sending the ball from one player to another, on ground or in air.

**PASUCKQUAKKOHOWOG:** Native American name for early version of soccer, played before Pilgrims arrived at Plymouth Rock; means "they gather to play football."

**PELE:** Brazilian; considered the greatest soccer player

**PAN AMERICAN GAMES:** Held every four years, during summer preceding Olympic Games, for countries in North, Central, and South America, and the Caribbean. Men's soccer has been part of every Pan American Games since inception in 1959; women's soccer debuted in Winnipeg, 1999. The United States sends U-23 national men's team, and full women's team.

**PARLOW, CINDY:** U.S. women's national team player; only player besides Mia Hamm to win back-to-back Hermann Trophies and Missouri Athletic Club ever. Burst upon scene in 1958 as 17-year-old World Cup star, then led his country to unprecedented three World Cup championships before retiring in 1973. Came out of retirement in 1975 to sign with New York Cosmos of North American Soccer League for $4.5 million; move gave league instant credibility. When he retired for a second time in 1977, Pele had set virtually every scoring record, and thrilled billions of soccer fans with creative brilliance and genuinely humble manner. "Pele" is nickname of unclear origins. Later served as Brazil's Minister of Sport. Elected to U.S. National Soccer Hall of Fame, 1993.

**PENALTY AREA (also called "Penalty box"):** Area (44 yards wide, 18 yards long) in which goalkeeper is allowed to use hands. Any direct kick foul committed inside penalty area is taken as penalty kick.

**PENALTY KICK:** When a direct kick foul is committed by defensive team in penalty area, offensive team is awarded penalty kick. Any member of offensive team may take shot, from penalty spot 10 yards from goal. Kicker faces goalkeeper, who may move laterally but not forward until ball is kicked. All other players on both teams remain outside box, at least 10 yards from shooter. At referee's signal, penalty kick is taken. If ball is saved, or strikes goalpost and rebounds onto field, it is still in play; however, shooter may not touch ball until another player on either team has touched it at least once.

**PENALTY KICK TIE-BREAKER:** Method of resolving tie games, in situations where there must be a winner (for example, tournaments). Each team designates five shooters, who alternate taking penalty kicks. Team that scores most penalty kicks wins. If both teams are still tied after five kicks, tiebreaker continues, with one from each team shooting until winner is decided.

Pele and England's Bobby Moore Exchange Shirts
after the 1970 World Cup Match

**PENALTY SHOT:** See "penalty kick."

**PENALTY SPOT:** Mark 12 yards from goal where penalty kicks are taken.

**PENNANT:** Often triangular, representing club or nation; customarily exchanged between captains at start of international or tournament matches.

**PETIT, EMMANUEL:** French midfielder; helped lead country to 1999 World Cup title.

**PHILIPS SV EINDHOVEN:** In 1988, as PSV Eindhoven, became one of only four clubs to win "triple crown" (league, F.A. Cup, and European championship in one season). Owned by Philips, the giant Dutch electronics company.

**PINNIES:** Mesh pullover vests used in training sessions to differentiate one group of players from another.

**PITCH:** English term for soccer field.

**PLANT FOOT:** Nonkicking foot; "planted" firmly on the ground, provides balance for kicker.

**PLATINI, MICHEL:** Midfield star of the 1970s and '80s, considered the greatest French player in history. In 1984, scored nine goals in five games to help France win European Cham-

1998 World Cup Final, Emmanuel Petit and Leonardo (Brazil)

pionship at home. As national team coach, took France to finals of 1992 European Championship; later helped organize World Cup '98.

**PLAYER DEVELOPMENT OPPORTUNITY (PDO):** Part of U.S. Soccer's Project 2010 (see below); aims to take 60 players each year, ages U-13 to U-21, and train them intensely 100 days a year (total of 1,000 players by 2010). Residency program began in January 1999 with U-17 boys' national team in Bradenton, Florida.

**PLAYING UP:** Playing in an age group higher than one's present age (a U-15 player on a U-17 team "plays up" two years).

**"PLAY ON!":** Shouted by referee, to indicate he has seen foul, and determines that stopping play would unfairly

Michel Platini

penalize team that was fouled against (because they are on the attack). Alternatively, "Play on!" means referee saw what could be considered an infraction, but in his judgment is not; in other words, he wants players to continue playing.

**POLAND:** Soccer heyday was in four-year span in the 1970s: won Olympic gold medal (1972), finished third at '74 World Cup, finished second at '76 Olympics.

**POOL (STATE, REGIONAL, OR NATIONAL):** Talented youth players are often selected to state, regional, or national team from "pool" of identified players. Pool players train together, but not all are chosen for team itself.

**POPE, EDDIE:** U.S. national team defender; scored in overtime to give D.C. United first MLS Cup championship. Current MLS team: D.C. United.

**PORTUGAL:** High-water mark was the 1960s, when players from great Benfica team made up bulk of national team; finished third at 1966 World Cup.

**POSSESSION:** When one team controls the ball, it is said to be "in possession." Possession is a key to soccer; team that does not possess the ball cannot score.

**PRACTICE SESSION:** Exactly what it sounds like. Included here, however, because phrase is going out of style. Preferred term is "training session."

**PREKI:** First made a name for himself in indoor soccer. Current MLS team: Kansas City Wizards.

**PREMIER DEVELOPMENT LEAGUE:** Part of United Soccer Leagues (USL); highest national amateur men's league in the United States.

**PREMIER LEAGUE:** Top division of English League soccer. Next lower division is actually called "First Division."

**PREMIER SOCCER:** In youth soccer, high level of travel competition. In some areas of the United States, this is the highest level of soccer before the Olympic Development Program.

**PRINCETON UNIVERSITY:** With Rutgers, played in first U.S. intercollegiate soccer match, November 6, 1876 (Rutgers won, 6–4).

**PROJECT-40:** Part of U.S. Soccer's Project 2010 (see below). Established in 1997 Project-40 allows promising players to bypass college and begin training in professional environment at an early age, 11 months each year. Included are seven months training with Major League Soccer teams; games are played with MLS squad, or A-League's Project-40 Select team.

**PROJECT 2010:** U.S. Soccer's plan to lift U.S. soccer into upper echelon of world soccer by 2010. Plan includes hosting and winning 2010 World Cup; and enhancing player development, administrative support, training facilities, coaching, and refereeing.

**PROMOTION:** Practice in many professional leagues around the world of promoting top one (or more) clubs from lower division into the next higher division for following year.

**PUNT:** Goalkeeper kick, following a save.

**"PUSH UP!":** Command given to defenders to move up, away from goal; objective is to initiate offense, and perhaps also catch opposition offside.

**PUSKAS, FERENC:** Hungarian star of the 1950s; nicknamed "The Little General." Keyed incredible 6–3 victory over England at Wembley (1953). Lethal left-footed inside forward. In 1962 played in World Cup for Spain, the country to which he defected after Hungarian Revolution of 1956.

## THE WORLD'S GREATEST GAMES
## 1982

**World Cup semifinal: West Germany 3, France 3 (West Germans win on penalty kicks, 5–4, after thrilling seesaw battle that includes vicious, but uncalled, foul by German keeper Schumacher)**

**QUEIROZ, CARLOS:**
Portuguese coach hired by U.S. Soccer to examine state of the game in this country, and suggest improvements. "Queiroz Report," released prior to World Cup 1998, detailed a blueprint for American soccer success in the 21st century.

# So, you think you know about soccer...

How many pentagons made up the official World Cup soccer ball of France '98 (the "Tricolore")?

A.  32
B.  28
C.  12
D.   6

Answer: A. And what do the pentagons do? Help control the ball in flight.

**RAMOS, TAB:** Veteran U.S. national team player (1990, '94, '98 World Cups); midfielder with great technical ability and creativity. First player to sign with Major League Soccer (1995). Has suffered several severe knee injuries, but always comes back. Current MLS team: New York/New Jersey MetroStars.

**RAMSAY, SIR ALF:** One of England's greatest coaches, who masterminded his nation's only World Cup championship (1966); national team coach, 1963–73. After a distinguished playing career as defender, shocked the world in 1963 by predicting England would win the Cup they were hosting in three years. Ramsay changed style of team, changing from five forwards to two, and "wingless wonders" succeeded. Led by Bobby Moore and Bobby Charlton, defeated West Germany 4–2 in overtime at Wembley. Knighted by the queen for World Cup coaching victory; dismissed as coach after World Cup qualifying failure against Poland in 1973. As a player, known as creative, intelligent right fullback with Southampton and Tottenham.

**RANGERS:** Glasgow club; with Celtic, half of one of international soccer's greatest rivalries. Long known as Glasgow's Protestant team. Won Scottish championship nine years in a row (1989–97).

**RAUL:** Spanish national team star; speedy forward, solid scorer. Full name: Raul Gonzalez. Current club team: Real Madrid (Spain).

**RAVELLI, THOMAS:** Star goalkeeper for Swedish

national team. Twin brother Andreas, a midfielder, also played on national team.

**REAL MADRID:** With Barcelona, half of Spain's top two teams. King Alfonso XIII added "Real" ("Royal") to original club name "Madrid" in honor of their many championships. Famous players include Alfredo Di Stefano, Ferenc Puskas, and Didi. Home stadium: Bernabeu.

**RECREATIONAL SOCCER:** Least competitive form of soccer. Most youngsters start out playing recreational ("rec") soccer; some move on to travel soccer, while others remain at this level. Little pressure to win; teams are balanced as evenly as possible, and rules often mandate that every player participate at least half of each match. Also called "in-house" soccer.

**RED CARD:** Signifies ejection of a player or coach by the referee; considered highest form of punishment in a soccer match. Red card can be given for violent and egregious fouls, or particularly bad

sportsmanship. Usually follows yellow card (warning), but warning need not occur first. Many leagues mandate player receiving red card, or accumulating a certain number of red cards, must sit out additional matches. Player who receives red card may not be substituted. NOTE: In many leagues, players who receive two yellow cards in match must also leave the field. In that case, player may be replaced. Yellow and red card system came into effect because players and coaches who did not speak the same language as the referee were not always certain they had been warned.

**REENTRY:** Returning to a game after being substituted. Prohibited at top levels of soccer worldwide.

**REFEREE:** Man or woman in charge of soccer match (also called "ref" or "official"). Although some countries and leagues have experimented with two referees, most soccer matches are played with one referee and two linesmen (also called "assistant referees"). Word comes from person to whom players would "refer" when in doubt about play.

**REGIONAL TEAMS:** In U.S. youth soccer, step between "state" Olympic Development Program teams and the national team. U.S. Youth Soccer Association breaks country into four regions: I (Northeast), II (Midwest), III (Southeast), and IV (West). Players from state teams are selected for regional camps and teams; from there, may be chosen for national camps and teams.

**REGIS, DAVID:** Native of Martinique with American wife; qualified for American citizenship, and joined U.S. national team right before 1998 World Cup. Current club team: F.C. Metz (France).

**REGULATION TIME:** Length of a soccer game, unless overtime is played. At highest levels, regulation time is 90 minutes. Referee keeps time on field.

**RELEGATION:** Practice, around the world, of dropping lowest one (or more) clubs in a soccer league into next lower division for following season. This ensures that even late-season games between weak clubs will be competitive and interesting.

**REP, JOHNNY:** Star of great Dutch teams in the 1970s.

**RESERVE:** Player who is not one of the original 11 starters (also called "substitute"). At top levels of play, there is a limited number of substitutes; at younger levels, unlimited substitution.

**FUN SOCCER FACTS**

U.S. national team player David Regis's first visit to the United States came in October 1994.

**RESERVE TEAM (also called "Reserve side"):** In international club soccer, the squad one level below top team (equivalent in U.S. baseball terms to a "farm team").

Bryan Robson and A. Gray

**RESTART:** When ball goes out of play, game begins with a "restart." Restarts include throw-ins, goal kicks, and corner kicks. Kickoff following a goal is also called a restart.

**REYNA, CLAUDIO:** U.S. national team midfielder. One of only three U.S. players to play every minute in 1998 World Cup; also played in 1994 World Cup. First American ever to captain a team in Europe (Wolfsburg, 1998). Current club team: Glasgow Rangers.

**RIJKAARD, FRANK:** Dutch star of the late 1980s and '90s; starred with great AC Milan club teams as well. Versatile midfielder and defender.

**RIMET, JULES:** President of FIFA and French federations during the 1920s; first World Cup trophy named in his honor.

**RIVALDO:** Brazilian national team star; stellar passer, play maker, and left-footed kicker. Scored three goals at World Cup '98; named to All-Tournament team. In 1999 called "best player in the world" by Pele. Full name: Victor Borba Ferreira. Current club team: Barcelona (Spain).

**RIVELINO:** Brazilian star of the 1970s, known for wondrous free kicks and corner kicks. Started career as left-winger; later became central midfielder. Credited unofficially with fastest goal in history (three seconds: shot from starting pass after noticing goalkeeper still concentrating on prematch prayers).

**RIVER PLATE:** Among most famous of Buenos Aires's 13 professional clubs, and one of the world's most famous.

**ROBERTO CARLOS:** Brazilian national team star; chunky defender known for powerful offense, and strong left foot. Scored memorable 40-yard free kick at World Cup '98. Helped current club team, Spain's Real Madrid, win UEFA Champions' League title in 1998. Full name: Roberto Carlos da Silva.

**ROBSON, BRYAN:** English midfield star of the 1980s and early '90s; known for suffering many broken bones.

**ROCHESTER RAGING RHINOS:** Most successful U.S. non-MLS pro team. Since formation in 1966, has averaged over 10,000 fans per game in A-League.

**ROMANIA:** Beginning in the late 1980s, became important force in European soccer; most top players now play abroad.

**ROMARIO:** Star of Brazil's 1994 World Cup–winning team; injury forced him off roster just days before 1998 World Cup. Like many modern Brazilians, made his club name in Europe (with PSV Eindhoven, Barcelona,

**World Cup Final Italy and Brazil: Romario with Trophy**

Valencia). Current team: Flamengo (Brazil).

**RONALDO:** Brazilian national team star with shaved head; named FIFA's World Player of the Year in 1996, at 20 years old. After year with Barcelona, contract was purchased by Inter Milan for $56 million; news made headlines throughout the world. However, pressure got to Ronaldo at the 1998 World Cup; he collapsed with what appeared to be anxiety attack just prior to finals against France. He played but was ineffective, and France pulled off upset victory. Nevertheless, he was awarded Golden Ball as top player of the tournament. Full name: Ronaldo Luiz Nazario da Lima. Current club team: Inter Milan (Italy).

**ROSE BOWL:** Stadium in Pasadena, California, which was the site of two of most famous games in soccer history, both decided by penalty kicks: 1994 World Cup final (won by Italy) and 1999 Women's World Cup final (won by host the United States). Both events drew more than 90,000 fans.

**ROSSI, PAOLO:** Italian star of the 1970s and '80s. Returned in spectacular fashion to 1982 World Cup, following two-year suspension for bribery scandal; scored hat trick against Brazil in wild 3–2 game, then twice more in 2–0 semifinal win over Poland,

Ronaldo

## FUN SOCCER FACTS

On September 5, 1885, Arbroath beat Bon-Accord 36–0 in the first round of the Scottish F.A. Cup. Winger John Petrie scored 13 goals, still a British record.

founder and chairman of Major League Soccer; previously commissioner of soccer for 1984 Olympic Games in Los Angeles. MLS championship trophy now called Alan I. Rothenberg Trophy. Practicing attorney; lives in Los Angeles.

**ROTH, WERNER:** One of the first American stars in North American Soccer League; elected to U.S. National Soccer Hall of Fame, 1989.

and once in 3–1 final victory over West Germany. Retired at 29.

**ROTE, KYLE, JR.:** With Ricky Davis, first American-born soccer star of the 1970s; gained fame with Dallas Tornado (NASL), and through impressive performances in ABC-TV's "Superstars" competitions.

**ROTHENBERG, ALAN:** As 1990–98 president of U.S. Soccer, and chairman and CEO of World Cup USA 1994, American soccer's premier figure in the 1990s. Also

**RUGBY:** Early in 19th century England, the game was very similar to soccer. Two games diverged when rule makers decided rugby players could hold and pass the ball with hands. Soccer ("football") players, of course, could not.

**RUMMENIGGE, KARL-HEINZ:** West German attacking star of the 1970s and early '80s. Captain of 1982 World Cup team; when West Germany lost to Italy, critics questioned whether injured Rummenigge should have been on field.

**RUSSIA (SOVIET UNION):** Strong national team in 1950s, led by goalkeeper Lev Yashin; however, besides winning first-ever European Championship (1960), Russia has won major title. In the 1970s and '80s, top players were Ukrainian; after breakup of Soviet Union, Russian national team suffered.

**RUTGERS UNIVERSITY:**
With Princeton, participant
in first U.S. intercollegiate
soccer match, November 6,
1876; Rutgers won, 6–4.

**SALAS, MARCELO:** Chilean national team star and captain; one of the world's leading strikers. Led River Plate to Argentine League title and named South American Footballer of Year, 1998. Nickname: "El Matador." Current club team: Lazio (Italy).

**SAMPSON, STEVE:** Head coach of U.S. national team, 1995–98; first U.S. coach in modern era to post winning record (26–22–14, .532 winning percentage). Resigned after dismal showing at World Cup '98, when the United States finished dead last of 32 teams. Born and raised in Southern California; began playing with American Youth Soccer Organization (AYSO) program.

**SACCHI, ARRIGO:** Italian national team coach in 1990s; earlier, head coach at AC Milan. His embrace of attacking soccer ended Italy's reliance on defense (*catenaccio*).

**SAINT LOUIS UNIVERSITY:** In 1959, winner of first National Collegiate Athletic Association (NCAA) men's soccer championship. In 1960, Billikens repeated as national champions; also won in 1962, '65, '66, '69, '72, and '73. Known for winning games with primarily St. Louis–born players.

**SAM'S ARMY:** Largest U.S. national team fan club; "Sam" stands for "Uncle Sam."

**SANCHEZ, HUGO:** Star of Mexican national team in the 1980s and early '90s; considered one of the country's greatest players ever. Top league scorer in Spain five seasons in a row. Celebrated each goal with a somersault.

**SAN JOSE CLASH:** Charter member of Major League Soccer (MLS).

**SANTOS:** Small São Paulo club with which Pele was associated for most of career. With Pele as centerpiece, Santos toured the world and drew sellout crowds.

**SAVE:** Preventing ball from going in goal; usually made by goalkeeper, although defenders can also save balls by clearing them off line.

**SCHELLSCHEIDT, MANNY:** Veteran U.S. college and youth coach; elected to U.S. National Soccer Hall of Fame, 1990.

**SCHEVCHENKO, ANDREI:** Young Ukrainian national team star; lethal forward. Debuted on international scene in 1997, sparking Dynamo Kiev through early rounds of UEFA Champions' League.

Current club team: AC Milan (Italy).

**SCHMEICHEL, PETER:** One of the top goalkeepers of the 1990s; burst on world scene in 1992 leading little-heralded Denmark to the European championship. In 1996 with Manchester United, 6–4 keeper played 1,135 minutes without surrendering goal. In 1999 in final appearance with United, went out winner as team won "triple." Current club team: Sporting Lisbon (Portugal).

Andrei Schevchenko

Peter Schmeichel

**SCHMID, SIGI:** American coach who scored resounding success with the University of California, Los Angeles; then, in 1999, moved after 19 years to Los Angeles Galaxy of Major League Soccer. Has coached several national youth teams, and served as national team assistant coach.

**SCHOEN, HELMUT:** Coach of West Germany's 1974 World Cup–winning team.

**SCHOLES; PAUL:** English national team star; stalwart attacking midfielder. Current club team: Manchester United.

**SCHUMACHER, HARALD:** West German goalkeeping star of the 1980s; best known for brutal (and uncalled) foul in 1982 semifinals against France. Without penalty kick call, West Germany went on to win in first penalty-kick World Cup game ever.

**SCISSORS KICK:** Made by a player with the body parallel to the ground; he or she "scissors" legs in the air. Often confused with "bicycle kick."

**SCOTLAND:** Despite small size, influential in international soccer (Scottish FA, founded 1873, still retains permanent seat on international board). Site of first international match, November 30, 1872; tied England 0–0. Many Scottish stars have played or coached England's most successful clubs. Known for determined national teams, and very supportive fans.

**SCRIMMAGE:** Practice game.

**SCURRY, BRIANA:** Goalkeeper for U.S. women's national team; starter since 1994. Saved penalty kick against China to help the United States win '99 title. Has three times more international starts than any other goalkeeper in U.S. history. Possesses amazing vertical leap.

**SELECT SOCCER:** One level up from recreation soccer. "Select" means players must be selected for a team, usually through tryout process. Select teams play coun-

terparts from other select clubs.

**SERIE A:** The top division of Italian soccer (literally, "Series A").

**FOOTNOTE:** Briana Scurry pledged to "run naked through the streets" if the United States won the gold medal at the 1996 Olympics. They did, and she did.

Briana Scurry

**SERVICE:** An accurate pass.

**SET PLAY:** Restart (corner kick or free kick) taken with definite plan of action in mind: for example, two players run over ball, and third strikes it short to fourth player. Also called "set piece."

**SHERINGHAM, TEDDY:** Manchester United player who came on as reserve late in 1999 European Cup final against Bayern Munich; scored and assisted on two injury time goals to give team amazing come-from-behind championship.

**SHIELDING:** Interposing the body between opponent and ball.

FOOTNOTE:
The U.S. women's national team has been active in the "Smoke Free Kids" program sponsored by the Department of Health and Human Services.

**SHILTON, PETER:** English goalkeeping star, known as perfectionist. Earned first cap at 20, last at 40 in 1990 World Cup. Conceded only 80 international goals.

**SHIN GUARDS:** Protective devices worn over shin, and under socks, to prevent injury. Once heavy and awkward, they have grown lighter over the years, and now are hardly even noticed. Also called "shin pads."

**SHINSPLINTS:** Pain in shins, caused by chronic running on hard surfaces; common soccer injury.

**"SHIRTS AND SKINS":** In training sessions and pickup games, easy way to determine one (male) team from another. One side wears shirts; the other does not.

**SHOOTOUT:** American invention for resolving tie games; first tried in North American Soccer League, now adopted by Major League Soccer. If game remains tied after overtime, five players participate in shootout. Alternating between each team, players start 35 yards from goal.

They dribble in, and have five seconds to shoot. Team that scores most shootout goals is awarded win (but with fewer points in standings than if it had won the match outright). If shootout remains tied after five attempts for each team, then one player from each side continues until winner is decided.

**SHORT-SIDED SOCCER (also called "Short goal"):** Training method using teams of small numbers of players, traditionally three, four, or five. Players compete on shortened field, and shoot on smaller goal—perhaps two cones or shirts placed on the ground. Short-sided soccer is good for developing individual and team skills in tight spaces, operating under pressure, and learning to play both offense and defense.

**SHOT:** An attempt to score; can be kicked, headed, or unintentionally deflected by member of either team.

# FUN SOCCER FACTS

When South Americans adopted the British sport of soccer, they also picked up the names of the most popular teams. That's why today there are teams named Corinthians in Brazil; Liverpool and Wanderers in Uruguay; Everton and Rangers in Chile; and Newell's Old Boys and River Plate in Argentina.

**SIDE:** A team (as in "the English national side").

**SIDELINE:** Line extending from one end of field to the other; also called "touch line." When ball is kicked over sideline ("out of touch"), opposing team restarts play with throw-in. Entire ball must be entirely over line to be considered out. On regulation-size field, sideline may be no shorter than 100 yards, no longer than 130 yards.

**SIDE VOLLEY:** Kick or shot made on a ball that is in the air, by extending foot across body.

**SISSI:** Brazilian women's national team star at 1999 World Cup; graceful, excellent on free kicks. Shaved head in emulation of Brazilian men's hero Ronaldo. Full name: Sisleide Lima do Amor.

**SLIDE TACKLE:** Defensive maneuver in which player attempts to win ball from opponent by sliding on ground, and kicking ball away.

**SMALL-SIDED SOCCER:** (see "Short-sided soccer").

**SNICKERS NATIONAL YOUTH CHAMPIONSHIP:** Series of 10 national titles for boys' and girls' youth teams (ages 16–20), organized by U.S. Youth Soccer Association.

**SOBRERO, KATE:** Central defender and rising star on U.S. women's national team. Defensive Most Valuable Player of 1995 NCAA tournament for national champion Notre Dame.

**SOCCER:** World's most popular game (duh); played in more countries than belong to the United Nations. Amazingly simple ball-and-goal game, with roots stretching back to ancient England, when entire villages played games involving balls made of pig's bladders or skulls of enemy soldiers. Modern version of soccer began in the 19th century, when Football Association in England met to develop unified set of rules. Currently the world's most popular sport, played by more than 150 million registered athletes (including 10 million women), enjoyed by billions of fans. 1998 World Cup drew 37 billion viewers, including 1.75 billion live viewers for final game. Name "soccer" is abbreviated version of "Association."

**SOCCER AMERICA:** Weekly soccer newsmagazine; leading soccer publication in the United States. Contact information: P.O. Box 23704, Oakland, CA 94623; tel.: (510) 528-5000; fax: (510) 528-5177; Web site: www.socceramerica.com.

**FOOTNOTE:** The average soccer player changes speed or direction every six seconds.

**SOCCER ASSOCIATION FOR YOUTH (SAY):** Affiliate member of U.S. Soccer Federation; over 6,500 recreational teams in seven age groups for boys and girls. Founded 1967. Contact information: 4903 Vine St., Suite 1, Cincinnati, OH 45217; tel.: (513) 242-4263; fax: (513) 482-7162.

**SOCCER INDUSTRY COUNCIL OF AMERICA:** Trade organization representing equipment and apparel manufacturers. Contact information: 200 Castlewood Dr., North Palm Beach, FL 33408; tel.: (561) 840-1171.

**SOCCER IN THE STREETS (SITS):** National nonprofit agency that develops soccer and educational programs for children in disadvantaged neighborhoods; operates in over 55 cities. Founded 1989. Contact information: 211 Porter La., Jonesboro, GA 30236; tel.: (770) 477-0354; fax: (770) 478-1862.

**SOCCER JUNIOR:** Bimonthly magazine aimed at young American soccer players ages 8–14. Contact information: 27 Unquowa Rd., Fairfield, CT 06430; tel.: (203) 259-5766; fax: (203) 256-1119.

**SOCCER START:** Program organized by U.S. Youth Soccer Association for young

South Africa

players in economically disadvantaged areas.

**"SOCCER WAR":** 1969 conflict between El Salvador and Honduras. After El Salvador won World Cup–qualifying match, army invaded Honduras on the pretext of protecting expatriate Salvadorean citizens. Death toll: 3,000.

**SOLSKJAER, OLE:** Manchester United player who came on as reserve late in 1999 European Cup final, then scored winning goal in overtime against Bayern Munich in amazing come-from-behind victory.

**SOSKIC, MILUTIN:** Goalkeeper coach, U.S. men's national team; made over 50 international appearances for Yugoslavia, including 1962 World Cup.

**SOUTH AFRICA:** Banned from international play for many years because of country's apartheid policy. South Africa has recently emerged as a power in African soccer (winner, African Nations Cup, 1996); introduction of black players into squad helped. Team nickname: Bafana Bafana.

**SOUTH AMERICAN FOOTBALL CONFEDERATION (CONMEBOL):** One of FIFA's six confederations; includes all South American soccer-playing nations. Contact information: tel.: 595-21-494-628; fax: 595-21-492-976; Web site: www.conmebol.com.

**SOUTH KOREA:** Although not a recognized soccer power, South Korea will cohost 2002 World Cup with Japan.

**"SPACE!":** Signal from one player to teammate with ball that he has plenty of space in front of him, and can turn and move quickly into it.

**SPAIN:** Hosted 1982 World Cup (won by Italy). Charter member of FIFA (1904). Most successful era: 1950s and '60s. Club teams (Barcelona, Real Madrid) have thrived using foreigners.

**SPECIAL OLYMPICS:** Organizes events, including soccer, for people with physical and mental disabilities. Contact information: tel.: (202) 628-3630; fax: (202) 824-0200.

**STADE DE FRANCE:** New 80,000-seat stadium built on the outskirts of Paris for 1998 World Cup; site of opening match and finals.

**STATE ASSOCIATION:** In the United States there are 55 state associations, all affiliated with the U.S. Soccer Federation (all 50 states have at least one association; five states have two). State associations are charged with registering youth players, developing coaches and referees, and regulating all soccer played within their borders.

**STATE TEAM:** Olympic Development Program (ODP) team that represents a particular state association in competition against other state teams, occasionally in international competition. Members of ODP team are said to be "on the state team."

**STEINBRECHER, HANK:** Secretary General (second in command) of U.S. Soccer. Previously vice-president of sports marketing for Quaker Oats (involved with Gatorade); also coached collegiately at Appalachian State and Boston University.

**STEPOVER:** Soccer move in which a player "steps over" the ball, attempting to fake out defender prior to touching ball with opposite foot.

**STEWART CUP (J. ROSS STEWART CUP):** Snickers National Youth Championship for girls' U-19 teams.

**STEWART, ERNIE:** Dutch native with American father; one of the fastest players on U.S. national team. Scored game-winner in 2–1 victory over Colombia that advanced the United States into second round at 1994 World Cup. Longtime star in Holland. Current club team: NAC Breda (Holland).

**STOICHKOV, HRISTO:** Bulgarian national team star

South America

of the 1990s; club team star with Barcelona.

**STONE CUP (ANDY STONE CUP):** Snickers National Youth Championship for boys' U-18 teams.

**STOPPER:** Specialized position on defense. Stopper plays in central defense, ahead of other defenders, and is charged with "stopping" (or at least slowing down and neutralizing) opposition's most dangerous offensive threat.

**STRIKER:** See "forward."

**STUDS:** Also called "cleats"; these are attached to bottom of soccer shoes, giving athletes traction on grass.

**SUAREZ, LUIS:** 1960s-era player; perhaps Spain's best player ever. One of the few Spaniards ever to play in Italy. Coached Spain at 1990 World Cup.

**SUBSTITUTE:** Player who is not one of original 11 starters (also called "reserve"). At top levels of play, there is a limited number of substitutes; at younger levels, unlimited substitution.

**SUDDEN DEATH:** Now called "golden goal"; goal scored in overtime that immediately ends a match.

**SUKER, DAVOR:** Croatian player; winner of Golden Boot as top scorer (six goals) at 1998 World Cup. Helped current club team, Real Madrid (Spain), win 1998 European Cup.

**SUPPORT:** Providing assistance to a player with ball, being close enough to pass to or act as a decoy. Support is usually provided both behind the player and laterally.

**SWARM BALL:** Style of play of young children, who "swarm" around soccer ball with little regard for positional play. Used derisively to describe older teams with little team concept.

**SWEATSHOPS:** Controversy in mid-1990s, when major soccer-ball manufacturers were found to be using child labor in Asia.

**SWEDEN:** One of the top women's soccer nations in the world; host of the 1995 Women's World Cup. Sweden hosted, and finished second at 1958 World Cup (won by Brazil, most notable for emergence of Pele on world scene). Charter member of FIFA (1904).

**SWEEPER:** Specialized defensive position. Sweeper's job is to "sweep" laterally, and stop or slow down any offensive player managing to breach defense. Position (also called "libero") was popularized by Franz Beckenbauer of Germany, who also went forward liberally after winning the ball.

**"SWITCH FIELDS!":** Command given to teammate to quickly move ball from one side of the field to the other; usually done with a long ball, but may be accomplished with two or three quick passes.

**SWITZERLAND:** Host of 1954 World Cup (won by West Germany). Charter member of FIFA (1904); now site (Geneva) of FIFA world headquarters.

**FOOTNOTE:** The U.S.-Switzerland game in the Pontiac, Michigan, Silverdome in 1994 was the first World Cup match ever played indoors.

**T**

**TABLE:** English term for "league standings."

**TACKLING:** Attempting to win the ball away from opponent with one's foot. Players can tackle while remaining on their feet, or by sliding on ground (see "slide tackle").

**"TAKE HIM ON!":** Command to attacking teammate to go one-on-one against defender.

**TAKEOVER:** Maneuver in which one player leaves ball for teammate to pick up on the run.

**TAMPA BAY MUTINY:** Charter member of Major League Soccer (MLS); had been expected to (but failed to) pick up mantle of successful Tampa Bay Rowdies of failed North American Soccer League.

**TARDELLI, MARCO:** Defender and midfield star of Italian national team in the 1980s. Won every major prize in game, including World Cup. Voted Man of the Match in 1982 World Cup final win over West Germany.

**TARGET:** Attacker who plays with his or her back to goal, and is "target" for teammates' passes. After receiving, "target player" can turn and attack self, or lay off pass for onrushing teammate.

**TEN:** Traditionally, jersey number worn by a team's top scorer; popularized by Pele.

**THIGH TRAP:** Controlling the ball by raising thigh to create flat "platform"; ball bounces from there to ground, or player's foot.

**THORNTON, ZACH:** Rising goalkeeper star on U.S. national team; replaced legendary Jorge Campos as keeper for Chicago Fire, named league Goalkeeper of Year as team won championship in inaugural year. Current MLS team: Chicago Fire.

**THROUGH BALL:** Pass that splits two defenders, in air or on ground.

**THROW-IN:** When ball is kicked or headed over sideline, opposing team is awarded throw-in. To be legal, throw-in must be taken with both feet on ground. Ball must come from behind head, and must be thrown, not dropped, into play.

**THURAM, LILLIAN:** French national team star; strong fullback with nose for goal (scored twice in 1998 World Cup semifinal against Croatia). Current club team: Parma (Italy).

**TIE-BREAKER:** Any method used to break tie games. In the United States, used in every Major League Soccer match that ends tied (see "shootout"). In rest of the world, tie-breakers are used only in tournament games that must produce a winner (for example, semifinal matches).

**"TIME!":** Signal from one teammate to another, indicating that player with ball (or about to receive it) is relatively unguarded, and has time to turn or make decision about what to do next.

**TIP SAVE:** Goalkeeper save, using fingertips to push ball out of danger.

**TITLE IX:** Federal law passed in 1972 mandating equal opportunities for females and males in educational, government-funded programs. Biggest impact has come in sports; credited with spurring growth of women's athletics, particularly soccer, in high schools and colleges around the United States.

**TOE POKE:** Knocking ball away with a lunge. Considered inelegant, but effective.

**TOPSOCCER:** Program for young players with disabilities; organized by U.S. Youth Soccer Association. Instruction and games include children without disabilities as well.

**TOSTAO:** "The White Pele"; Brazilian star in 1966 World Cup and, following surgery for detached retina, 1970 World Cup as well. Retired in 1973; became eye specialist.

**"TOTAL SOCCER":** Term given to style of soccer played by great Dutch teams of the 1970s. In "Total Soccer," players rotated positions constantly, moving up to attack and back to defend almost at will. Demanded highly skilled, very creative, and quite fit players, and coach who did not feel the need to fit players into set positions. Therefore, it was very difficult for other countries to duplicate.

**TOUCH:** Refers to either a player's comfort with ball ("she has a good touch"), or the sideline ("the ball went out of touch"). Can also be used as a command. ("Touch!" means "touch it once, then send it to me!")

**TOUCH LINE:** Line extending from one end of the field to the other; also called "sideline." When ball travels over sideline ("out of touch"), opposing team restarts play with throw-in. Entire ball must be entirely over line to be considered out. On regulation-size field, sideline may be no shorter than 100 yards, no longer than 130 yards.

**TRAILER:** Player who trails attacker with ball; usually unguarded, and can be used for back pass.

**TRAINER:** Refers either to coach who actively leads a training session, or to person who handles team's medical, health, and nutrition tasks.

**TRAINING SESSION:** See "practice session."

**TRANSITION:** Moving from offense to defense, or vice versa, whenever team gains or loses possession of the ball. "Transition game" is key to soccer; the quicker and more conscientious a team is during many transitions that occur each match, the more successful it will be.

**TRAP:** See "control."

**TRAVEL SOCCER:** In youth soccer, designates competitive teams and leagues. Teams travel beyond local towns to play matches and tournaments.

**TRINIDAD AND TOBAGO:** Tiny island nation in the Caribbean that for many years gave the United States great difficulty. Only late goal by Paul Caligiuri, for example, enabled the United States to beat Trinidad and Tobago and qualify for the 1990 World Cup.

**TRIPLE CROWN (also called "Triple" and "treble"):** Winning three major championships in one year (for example, in European soccer, the European Cup, and domestic league and cup titles). Four European teams have done it: Celtic (1967), Ajax (1972), PSV Eindhoven

**FUN SOCCER FACTS**

The 1998 World Cup was estimated to have a combined television audience of 37 billion people, including a record 1.75 billion for the final game.

(1988), and Manchester United (1999).

**TRIPPING:** Causing an opponent to lose balance. Tripping foul results in a direct kick for the other team.

**"TURN!":** Signal from one player to teammate that he should turn with the ball and move forward on attack.

U

**U-17 MEN'S NATIONAL TEAM, U.S.:** In 1999 team began training full-time in residency camp in Florida. the United States is the only country in the world to qualify for every U-17 World Championship since inaugural year, 1985.

**U-18 MEN'S NATIONAL TEAM, U.S.:** Intermediate program between more extensive U-17 and U-20 levels.

**U-18 WOMEN'S NATIONAL TEAM, U.S.:** Feeder program for U-21 team; formed 1998.

**U-:** Prefix used to designate age groups in soccer; stands for "Under," though it really means "up to." Thus, "U-14" ("Under-14") team is composed of players up to and including 14 years old.

**U-20 MEN'S NATIONAL TEAM, U.S.:** Has qualified for seven FIFA World Youth Championships since event's inception in 1977. Best finish: 4th (1989, in Saudi Arabia).

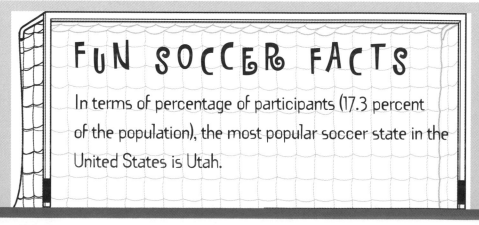

# FUN SOCCER FACTS

In terms of percentage of participants (17.3 percent of the population), the most popular soccer state in the United States is Utah.

**U-21 WOMEN'S NATIONAL TEAM, U.S.:** Formed in 1989; serves as development squad for full national team. Competes annually in Scandinavia's Nordic Cup, premier international U-21 tournament.

**U-23 MEN'S NATIONAL TEAM, U.S.:** Serves as men's Olympic team during Olympic qualifying and competition; also competes in Pan American Games. Current U.S. team consists primarily of professional players.

**UEFA (Union of European Football Associations):** One of FIFA's six confederations; includes all soccer-playing European nations. Contact information: tel.: 41-22-994-4444; fax: 41-22-994-4488.

**UEFA CUP:** Annual tournament among top club teams in Europe. In 2000, began with 121 clubs; another 24 added out of the Champions' League. Begun in 1958.

**UMPIRE:** Predecessor of "referee." In 1800s soccer used two "umpires," one chosen by each team's captain. Word comes from French ("single man"); in cricket, a single umpire was used.

**UNITED SOCCER ASSOCIATION (USA):** Professional league organized in 1967; merged at end of year with National Professional Soccer League to form North American Soccer League.

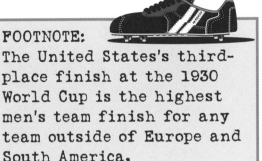

**FOOTNOTE:**
The United States's third-place finish at the 1930 World Cup is the highest men's team finish for any team outside of Europe and South America.

**UNITED SOCCER LEAGUES (USL):** Formerly United Systems of Independent Soccer Leagues (USISL); second tier of soccer in the United States, below Major League Soccer. After merging with A-League in 1996, USL includes 130 teams competing in the following leagues: A-League (Division II professional), D3 Pro League (Division III professional),

Premier Development League (national amateur), W-League (national women's amateur), and Y-League (national elite youth). Contact information: 14497 North Dale Mabry Hwy., Suite 201, Tampa, FL 33618; tel.: (813) 963-3909; fax: (813) 963-3807; Web site: www.unitedsoccerleagues.com.

**UNITED STATES AMATEUR SOCCER ASSOCIATION (USASA):** Adult (over 19) amateur division of United States Soccer Federation. Administers George F. Donnelly Cup (national championship for state select teams), as well as Over-30 Cup; in conjunction with U.S. Soccer Federation, stages U.S. Open Cup, and organizes U.S. Soccer Festival. Contact information: 7800 River Rd., North Bergen, NJ 07047; tel.: (201) 861-6277; fax: (201) 861-6341.

**UNITED STATES SOCCER FEDERATION (USSF):** Also called U.S. Soccer; national governing body for soccer in the United States. Over 100 employees based in Chicago headquarters. An affiliate of FIFA, USSF oversees U.S. soccer at all levels, from professional to youth; umbrella also covers coaches, referees, and administrators, and nine full national teams. USSF mission statement is to make soccer, in all forms, a preeminent sport in the United States, and to challenge for men's World Cup by 2010. In 1913 U.S. Soccer (then called United States Football Association; later, U.S. Soccer Football Association) became one of the world's first organizations to affiliate with FIFA. Hosted World Cup in 1994 (winner: Brazil), the most financially successful Cup ever. Also hosted and won Women's World Cup 1999. USSF registers 3 million youth players and 300,000 amateur adults; 80,000 coaches (10,000 are nationally licensed), and over 100,000 referees. USSF also sponsors coaching schools, where participants can gain certification in six progressive levels. Contact information: U.S. Soccer House, 1801 South Prairie Ave., Chicago, IL 60616; tel.: (312) 808-1300;

fax: (312) 808-1301; Web site: www.us-soccer.com.

**UNITED STATES SOCCER FESTIVAL:** Annual event involving four United States Amateur Soccer Association regional select teams, and one or two U.S. national team selections.

**UNITED STATES SOCCER FOUNDATION:** Nonprofit arm of U.S. Soccer, charged with disbursing profits from 1994 World Cup to youth and amateur organizations around the United States.

Since 1996, has allotted over $8 million to more than 100 entities in 38 states for field construction, programs for inner-city youth and physically challenged youngsters, etc. Contact information: 1050 17th St. NW, Suite 670, Washington, DC 20036; tel.: (202) 496-1292; fax: (202) 496-9669.

**UNITED STATES YOUTH SOCCER ASSOCIATION (USYSA):** Youth (ages 5–19) division of U.S. Soccer Federation, involving both recreational and competitive

## So, you think you know about soccer...

How much time in an average 90-minute match is spent moving backward?

A. 30 seconds
B. 1 minute
C. 5 minutes
D. 10 minutes

Answer: C

programs; approximately 3 million players and 300,000 coaches are registered, through 55 state associations. Encourages small-sided games for players under 10. USYSA runs Olympic Development Program, which identifies and develops top American players. Contact information: 899 Presidential Dr., Suite 117, Richardson, TX 75081; tel.: 1-800-4-SOCCER; fax: (214) 235-4480; Web site: www.usysa.org.

**UNIVERSITY OF NORTH CAROLINA:** One of the most remarkable dynasties in sports. Tar Heel women, under coach Anson Dorrance, won nine consecutive NCAA championships (1986–94), giving women's soccer a major boost. At one point, UNC had won more than 100 consecutive games.

**UNIVERSITY OF VIR-GINIA:** Men's college soccer dynasty. Cavaliers, coached by Bruce Arena, tied for NCAA Division I title in 1989, then reeled off four straight crowns (1991–94), using only American players.

**UNIVISION:** A Spanish-language U.S. television network known for its commitment to soccer broadcasting. Broadcaster Andreas Cantor's "Gooooooooooollllllll!!!!!!!!!!!!!" call is Univision signature.

**UNLIMITED SUBSTITU-TION:** In youth soccer, policy of allowing unlimited number of players to enter and reenter match. At higher levels, there is limited substitution: Only a certain number of substitutions is allowed, and a player who has left a match cannot reenter.

**"UNLUCKY!":** Popular saying of players, coaches, and fans. Can be uttered after any unfortunate event: missed shot, bad play by goalkeeper, dubious foul, illegal throw, whatever. Soccer's version of "too bad!"

**UNSPORTSMANLIKE CON-DUCT:** Covers a wide range of infractions, including improper language, attempting to seek advantage by "diving," etc. Punishable by indirect kick awarded to the other team.

**URUGUAY:** In 1930 site of first World Cup. Only 13 nations competed; all but four European nations chose not to make the long ocean voyage to South America. Successful event, as host Uruguayans won championship, 4–2 over Argentina. Some 93,000 fans packed stands for the final match. Became second team (after Italy) to win second World Cup championship, with 2–1 victory over Brazil in 1950. Uruguay also won 1928 Olympics. Tied with Argentina for most Copa America championships (14).

**U.S. CUP:** Four-team, six-game international tournament; most prestigious annual men's event conducted by U.S. Soccer Federation. The United States won inaugural title in 1992; repeated in 1995. Similar U.S. Women's Cup established in 1994; the United States has won every year it has been contested.

**U.S. OPEN CUP:** Oldest cup competition in U.S. soccer (1914); among the world's oldest. Open to all affiliated amateur and professional teams in the United States. Single-elimination tournament based on similar competitions played around the world, concurrent with domestic league action.

**U.S. SOCCER HOUSE:** Headquarters of United States Soccer Federation (USSF) in Chicago. Refurbished mansion in Prairie

# THE WORLD'S GREATEST GAMES
# 1999

European Cup final: Manchester United 2, Bayern Munich 1 (Two goals in injury time give "Man U" thrilling come–from–behind victory—and coveted "triple")

Avenue Historical District; has been featured as location shot in many motion pictures, including *Primal Fear.*

**USA CUP:** Youth tournament held annually in Blaine, Minnesota, on 56 contiguous fields; considered largest youth tournament in the United States.

## FUN SOCCER FACTS

Although modern soccer balls weigh an ounce more than earlier models, they seem lighter because of plastic coating and superior manufacturing techniques that prevent water retention.

**V:** In soccer world, stands for "versus." Thus, 3-v.-3 game (pronounced "three-vee-three") is short-sided game of three players against three players.

**VALDERRAMA, CARLOS:** Instantly recognizable by wild, red dreadlocks; captained Colombia's national team for a decade, and was twice named South American Player of the Year. When signed by Tampa Bay Mutiny in 1996, became one of Major League Soccer's first stars; won league's first-ever Most Valuable Player Award. Played briefly for Miami Fusion before returning to Tampa Bay.

**VAN BASTEN, MARCO:** Dutch star of the late 1980s and '90s. With Ajax and AC Milan, named FIFA, World, and European Player of the Year. Ankle injuries forced early retirement.

**VAN DER SAAR, EDWIN:** Dutch national team goalkeeper (one of the world's best); won numerous titles with Ajax. Current club team: Juventus (Italy).

**VASCO DA GAMA:** Rio de Janeiro club; one of the first in Brazil to use mixed-race players.

**VENTURINI, TISHA:** U.S. women's national team star; second-highest scoring midfielder in U.S. history. Named top college player in the country in 1994, as University of North Carolina senior.

**VERMES, PETER:** Longtime U.S. national team defensive stalwart. Current MLS team: Colorado Rapids.

**VERON, JUAN SEBASTIAN:** Argentine national team star; midfield general, excellent shooter. Named to 1998 World Cup All-tournament team. Shaved head. Current club team: Lazio (Italy).

**VIERI, CHRISTIAN:** Italian national team star; one of the world's top strikers. Played on four teams in four years; combined transfer fees totaled over $100 million. Second in scoring to Davor Suker at World Cup '98.

Current club team: Inter Milan (Italy).

**VIGNOTTO, ELISABETTA:** Italian female player from the 1970s and '80s who retired with 107 goals, at the time the most in soccer history.

**VOLLEY:** Shot struck before ball hits ground; extremely powerful, and difficult to execute.

## So, you think you know about soccer...

Which was the only World Cup without a final game?

A.  1930
B.  1934
C.  1950
D.  1958

Answer: C. The competition was arranged on a pool basis. Brazil, Uruguay, Sweden, and Spain all qualified for the final pool; host Brazil and Uruguay met in the last game, which acted as a final. All Brazil needed was a tie--but Uruguay won 1-0, and after 20 years were world champs again.

**WALL:** Defensive alignment to guard against free kick close to goal. Players line up shoulder to shoulder, denying kicker clear shot on goal. Walls may be set up by keeper or any other player; the closer the free kick is to the goal, and nearer to center of the goal, the more players should be put in wall.

**WALL PASS:** Pass in which one player acts as a "wall"; after receiving the ball, he immediately one-touches it to the player who gave it to him. Also called a "give-and-go," or a "one-two."

**WARM-UP:** Jogging, stretching, and kicking before a match or training.

**WARNING:** See "yellow card."

**WASHINGTON, DANTE:** College scoring sensation; currently plays for MLS Dallas Burn.

**WATFORD:** Small English club that in 1984 transfixed the world by progressing all the way to F.A. Cup final.

**WEAH, GEORGE:** Liberian national team star. In 1995 he became the only man ever named FIFA World Player of the Year, European Football Player of the Year, and African Football Player of the Year in the same year; also first African ever to win FIFA and European titles. Played in Europe in both French and Italian leagues; one of the world's greatest players never to appear in a World Cup. Also known as humanitarian for relief efforts in native land. Current club team: AC Milan (Italy).

**WEBBER, SASKIA:** Goalkeeper on U.S. national team; starter in 1993, recently made comeback.

**WEMBLEY:** Located in London; English soccer shrine, and one of the world's most famous soccer stadiums. Hosted 1966 World Cup final, 1948 Olympic final, most F.A. Cup finals. Capacity: 80,000.

**WEN SUN:** Chinese women's national team star; great dribbler, creative play maker, key scorer at 1999 World Cup. At 18, started all four games when China hosted 1991 World Cup.

**WEST GERMANY:** Won 1954 World Cup in Switzerland, with 3–2 victory over Hungary. Hosted 1974 World Cup; won championship at home, 2–1 over Holland. Won third World Cup championship in 1990, 1–0 over Argentina in Italy. Three-time World Cup runners-up: 1966 (4–2 to England, in overtime); 1982 (3–1 to Italy), 1986 (3–2 to Argentina). (See also "Germany.")

**WIEGMANN, BETTINA:** German women's national team star; defensive midfielder adept at winning ball and initiating attacks. Named 1997 Player of the Year in Germany.

**WING:** Outside part of field; also called "flank." "Wing" also referred, through the 1960s, to actual forward positions ("left wing" and "right wing").

**W-LEAGUE:** U.S. women's national league (amateur); part of United Soccer Leagues (USL).

**"WM" SYSTEM:** First major tactical formation of five attackers, two midfielders, and three defenders; so-called because diagram looks like "W" in offensive half of the field, "M" on defense.

**WOMEN'S SOCCER:** Explosive growth in the United States has helped women's game progress around the world. In the United States, 7.5 million female players are registered. Game is popular at all levels, from youth leagues to college and national team.

**WOMEN'S WORLD CUP:**
Event began in 1991 as Women's World Championship; renamed Women's World Cup in 1999. the United States won inaugural event in China in 1991, beating Norway 2–1 in front of 60,000 fans on two goals by Michelle Akers. In Sweden in 1995 the United States finished third; Norway won. In 1999, the United States hosted the Women's World Cup for the first time and won the title in dramatic fashion, 5–4 on penalty kicks over China following 120 minutes of a 0–0 draw. Sixteen teams participated; all 32 matches were televised in the United States. More than 90,000 fans attended final at the Rose Bowl, the largest crowd ever to witness a women's sporting event anywhere. Observers called that U.S. championship, and America's embrace of women's team, a defining event in women's sports in the world.

# So, you think you know about soccer...

How much time in an average 90-minute match is spent moving backward?

A.    30 seconds
B.    1 minute
C.    5 minutes
D.    10 minutes

Answer: C

Concaff Gold Cup '98
Eric Wynalda and
Juan C. Llorente (Cuba)

**WOOSNAM, PHIL:** Founder and commissioner, North American Soccer League; elected to U.S. National Soccer Hall of Fame, 1997.

**WORLD CHAMPIONSHIPS:** Only men's and women's full national team championships are called World Cups; they are contested every four years. U-20 and U-17 tourna- ments, held every two years, called simply World Championships. Also contested: Fụtsal World Championship, won all three times it was held (1989, '92, '96) by Brazil.

**WORLD CLUB CUP:** Challenge match between club champions of Europe and South America; begun in 1960.

**WORLD CUP:** Most prestigious sports tour- nament in the world. Held every four years since 1930 (except 1942 and 1946, because of World War II); attracts scores of teams, billions of television viewers. Historically, Brazil, Italy, and Germany have been the most successful World Cup teams. The United States hosted World Cup in 1994, appeared in the first two World Cups (1930, '34); also appeared in 1950, record- ing astonishing 1–0 win over England. Next appearance did not come for 40 years; since then, one of only 12 teams to appear in all three World Cups (1990, '94, and '98).

**WORLD PLAYER OF THE YEAR:** Award voted on by national team coaches throughout the world, was inaugurated in 1990; sponsored by FIFA.

**WORLD YOUTH CHAMPIONSHIP:** Called informally "Youth World Cup"; international competitions held every two years for U-17 and U-20 teams.

**WORTMANN, IVO:** Head coach, Major Soccer League Miami Fusion; assistant coach, U.S. men's national team. Previous coaching experience: Saudi Arabia, Qatar, United Arab Emirates, Brazil.

**WYNALDA, ERIC:** All-time leading scorer for U.S. national team; three-time World Cup veteran (1990, '94, '98). Scored first goal in MLS history, later called Goal of the Year. Current MLS team: Miami Fusion.

**FUN SOCCER FACTS**

The only two U.S. national team soccer players to appear on the cover of *Sports Illustrated* are Ernie Stewart (June 1994) and Brandi Chastain (July 1999).

referee following repeated or flagrant fouls. Expectation is that behavior will cease; if it continues, referee may issue second yellow card (ejection, although player may be replaced) or red card (ejection without replacement). Yellow and red card system came into effect because players and coaches who did not speak the same language as the referee were not always certain they had been warned.

**YASHIN, LEV:** Russian with long arms and quick reflexes, considered by many the greatest goalkeeper ever. Helped his country win first European championship in 1960, four years after capturing gold medal at 1956 Olympics. Also known for great sportsmanship. Nickname: "The Black Spider."

**YEAGLEY, JERRY:** Veteran Indiana University soccer coach; elected to U.S. National Soccer Hall of Fame, 1989.

**YELLOW CARD:** Warning issued to player or coach by

**Y-LEAGUE:** National league for elite youth players; part of the United Soccer Leagues (USL).

**"YOU'LL NEVER WALK ALONE":** Famed anthem of Liverpool team.

**YOUTH NATIONAL TEAMS, U.S.:** U.S. Soccer Federation sponsors national teams at men's U-20, U-18, and U-17 levels, and women's U-20 level. The United States U-17s and Australia are only two countries to qualify for every U-17 World Championship since inception in 1985.

**YUGOSLAVIA:** Known for producing great players and coaches who play abroad, but weak national teams.

Yugoslavia

**Z**

Minister of Sport, moved to Japan to help launch J-League in 1993.

**ZIDANE, ZINADINE:** Star of France's 1998 World Cup–winning team, and 1998 FIFA World Player of the Year award for attacking midfield play; scored twice on headers in France's 3–0 final victory over Brazil. Top-ranked play maker in the world, with dynamic dribbling skills and superb finishing ability. In 1998 he also led his club team, Juventus, to Italian League title. Son of Northern African immigrants; nickname: Zizou. Current club team: Juventus (Italy).

**ZAGALO, MARIO:** Coach of Brazil's 1970 World Cup–winning team.

**ZELMO:** Soccer's version of "horse." Juggling game used in warm-ups; a player who misjuggles is given a letter. First player to spell "Zelmo" loses.

**ZENGA, WALTER:** Italian goalkeeper; player-coach of MLS team New England Revolution.

**ZICO:** Brazilian star in the 1970s and '80s; best performance was at 1982 World Cup. After serving as Brazil's

**ZIEGE, CHRISTIAN:** German national team star; midfielder/defender. Helped lead Germany to 1996 European championship, and Milan to Serie A title 1999. Current club team: AC Milan (Italy).

**ZOFF, DINO:** Italian goalkeeper throughout 1980s; star of 1982 World Cup–winning team. Earned 112 caps. On negative side, known for excessive time-wasting, which led to rules changes that speeded up game.

**ZONE MARKING:** Defensive tactic in which each defender covers a certain area, or "zone," of the field.

Zinadine Zidane

## PHOTO CREDITS